HOW TO LEAD WITH

Emotional

INTELLIGENCE

HOW TO HANDLE YOUR EMOTIONS
ACCORDING TO GOD'S WORD

LEEANAH JAMES

Acknowledgements

Thank you, God, for the years of working with me, and loving me, and saving me. Thank you for the spiritual gifts you have given me and the support you have placed in my life. This has been a beautiful process.

Kristian- My love, my partner, my best friend. Thank you for your support. Never complaining about my late night, and early morning writing sessions. Thank you for encouraging me to shine bright, you are my hero!

Mom and Dad- Thank you for being my biggest cheerleaders throughout life. My confidence in Christ stems largely from your answered prayers.

Mother in Love - Your belief in me is so encouraging. You root for me as if you birthed me and you are willing to fight with me for me. I see you mom and I appreciate you.

Aunt Monica- Thank you for all the encouragement, books on writing and prayers. I felt them from Canada!

Summer, Kristian II, and Autumn Reign - Thank you for all the beautiful content you add to the story of my life.

Diamond- Girl, you really came through for me during this time. Thank you so much! I am so glad you are my sister in Christ!

Natalie- I didn't know how much I needed your help with this, until you provided it. You are AMAZING!

Leila- Thank you for the encouragement and the many hours of reading and feedback you provided. I love you.

Mi'Lisa- Thank you for the constant encouragement. It always seemed to come on the days when I needed it the most. You have no idea how much good your messages, hugs, prayers and encouragement has helped me.

Melannie- Thank you for the "heart checks" it made me pause throughout the process and do some self-care. I love you girl!

Preface

Emotional Intelligence is a business concept developed by Stanley Greenspan in 1989. Years later psychologist and businessmen began to share their ideas on the topic. Businessmen and women explore these ideas in the workplace, however, these types of ideas aren't always presented in a way that easily translates to practical and spiritual ministry.

You may be wondering, "What exactly is Emotional Intelligence and why would I need to implement these concepts and techniques as a church leader?" Simply put, Emotional Intelligence is the ability to control one's own emotions as well as the ability influence the emotions of others.

There are five components of Emotional Intelligence:

- Self-awareness
- Self-regulation
- Motivation
- Empathy
- Relationships

Church leaders and members can utilize this biblically sound concept, to strategically and intentionally reach the world for Christ and build the Kingdom of God.

I believe the Bible is the Word of God. It is true, unwavering, and it is the standard for my life, so when adopting new concepts, ideas, or mindsets it is wise to measure it against the one thing I know to be unchanging. This book will explore what the Bible says about these five components of Emotional Intelligence and how we should govern our lives as a result.

In this book you will discover how these concepts can impact your life through intentional application and prayer. Each component of emotional intelligence is examined and explained with both the individual and local church in mind. This is a faith-based book written to encourage and uplift you on your life's journey.

Please take the time out to apply these techniques to your life by partnering with a group or partner to answer the questions at the end of each chapter. I pray your life is truly impacted by applying the Word of God to your everyday life through these concepts.

Table of Contents

CHAPTER 1

Self-Awareness

Self-awareness is the ability to honestly look at and identify how you feel. This may seem simple, until you have to determine if you are frustrated or angry, angry or disappointed; disappointed or just disillusioned. When I am frustrated it is usually linked to my inability to do something to affect the change I want to see. It is the emotional struggle between what I want to happen and what is actually happening. When I am angry, it is usually tied to something I cannot control or remedy. It is an emotional response to something that has or is happening regardless of my response.

It is important to know how you are feeling, and why you are feeling that way, so you can act appropriately. For example, if I am frustrated, based on my personal definition, there is likely something I can do to alter the circumstance. Identifying that what I feel is frustration and not anger helps determine my next move. It serves as a reminder that a remedy is not out of my hands.

To determine how I feel I often have to stop and ask myself these four questions.

1. How do I feel?
2. When did I start feeling this way?
3. Why do I feel this way?
4. How do I feel?

The first question "How do I feel?" is to place you in the mindset of putting a name to your feeling. Once you name that feeling, you have control over it. The second question, "When did I start feeling this way?" determines your influences. What was going on at the time your emotion changed? This can also help you re-create environments to elicit positive emotion. If you feel peace whenever you are sitting by moving water, then it is likely that sitting by moving water evokes feelings of peace for you.

The third question, "Why do I feel this way?" helps you identify the specific thing that happened at the point your emotion changed. It is not the timing of the incident but rather dissecting the incident itself. Finally, the answer the last question, "How do I feel?" is likely your true emotion. In some cases, this answer does not change, but in many cases, it does. The more you practice self-awareness the more likely the answers to the first and last questions will be the same.

Let me give you a personal example.

How do I feel?
I am frustrated.

When did I start feeling this way?
This morning the kids wouldn't sit and eat their breakfast and wanted to play instead after crying and saying they were hungry.

Why do you feel this way?
Because, I was up all night with the baby and I could have rested a little longer while the kids played in the playroom. Instead I got up to fix the breakfast they don't want to sit and eat.

How do I feel?
I am tired.

In this example I can say I was frustrated but the real feeling behind my emotion was exhaustion. Self-realization is getting to as close to the true feeling as possible.

Self-awareness also helps you effectively share how you are feeling with others. For example, you may feel lonely instead of sad. Your loneliness can also make you feel sad. One emotion can lead you to another. Once you regulate that first emotion, subsequent emotions will line up with the change.

As a believer, it is important that we don't buy into the lie of having it "all together" all the time. God knows our hearts. He knows the innermost details of our being, so He is not surprised or disappointed by our feelings. He knows all, so we might as well tell Him all. One of my favorite songs is sung by Hillary Scott. She opens the song with these words:

> "I'm so confused
> I know I heard you loud and clear
> So, I followed through
> Somehow, I ended up here
> I don't wanna think
> I may never understand
> That my broken heart is a part of your plan
> When I try to pray
> All I've got is hurt and these four words
> Thy will be done"

"Thy Will Lyrics." *Lyrics.com.* STANDS4 LLC, 2018. Web. 2 Mar. 2018. <https://www.lyrics.com/lyric/32873016>.

God is not asking that we no longer feel when we give our lives to Him. He is not asking that we become lemmings void of feeling simply following commands. He simply asks us that when everything in us is screaming against His word and His will that we simply surrender. He is asking for unrelenting trust; to take that one step, and another, and another. He doesn't mind us checking for His presence or seeking His reassurance.

Matthew 14:25-29 reads,

> [25] Now in the fourth watch of the night Jesus went to them, walking on the sea.

> [26] And when the disciples saw Him walking on the sea, they were troubled, saying, "It is a ghost!" And they cried out for fear.

> [27] But immediately Jesus spoke to them, saying, "Be of good cheer! It is I; do not be afraid."

> [28] And Peter answered Him and said, "Lord, if it is You, command me to come to You on the water."

> [29] So He said, "Come." And when Peter had come down out of the boat, he walked on the water to go to Jesus. 30 But when he saw that the wind was boisterous,[b] he was afraid; and beginning to sink he cried out, saying, "Lord, save me!"

I love that when the disciples yelled out in fear Jesus did not dismiss them as silly or overreacting. He did not mock them or down play the level of emotion they exhibited. He simply said, "Be of good cheer! It is I; do not be afraid." In other words, "Be happy! I'm here!" Peter immediately tested the spirit. "God if that is you command me to come to You on the water." Jesus said, "Come."

I believe Peter was still afraid. He asked Jesus to verify who He was in the context of their relationship. If you are who you say you are, then you tell me to come to you. When Jesus said, "Come." He created the atmosphere where Peter was able to step out onto the water and walk to Him. As long as Peter was focused on Jesus the atmosphere for him to do the impossible remained intact. When I was a kid there was a saying, "You're not Jesus, you can't walk on water." If I knew then what I know now my bold response would have been, "No but I have faith like Peter!"

As we continue reading the passage we see that Peter allowed outside forces to break his focus on Jesus and he began to sink. The thing is

Peter was a fisherman. He could swim. When we allow outside forces to break our focus on Jesus, the enemy will use our feelings to convince us we can't do something we know we can. Had Peter identified and called out his feelings, and refocused his mind on Jesus he would have been able to pick himself up and walk on the water again.

Thank God that when we are not operating in the mindset to be able to pick ourselves up out of deep and rough waters that we serve a God who will reach down and pick us up out of the situation we are drowning in. He knows how to properly identify every one of our emotions.

Self-awareness is the foundation of not only Emotional Intelligence, but of our faith. ***Recognizing our need for a savior is self-awareness at its fullest.*** When we come to God asking for salvation it is through self-awareness that we recognize our need for a savior.

Jesus shows us the importance of self-awareness in Matthew 26:39. He cries out to the father asking if the cup of pain, suffering, and bearing the sins of all mankind could be taken from Him. Jesus allowed Himself to feel the fear and anxiety any human would feel in that situation. He acknowledged his feelings before he continued with the difficult task at hand. As Christians Jesus is our standard for behavior. *"If this cup can pass from me. Yet not as I will but as you will."*

I love that Jesus fully took on being human. He did not have to share with us his struggle of going to Calvary. Jesus could have easily carried his cross, walked up onto that hill and died. Instead he bore the full weight of our sins. He felt every ounce of our discretions and He accepted the bitter cup of pain for our sakes. Even his plea to have the cup passed from Him was done with us in mind.

I believe Jesus intended to show us that he understands emotions and He can truly relate to how we feel. Jesus was self-aware. We should follow suit by honestly communicating how we feel and what we desire the response to our feelings to be. Self-awareness is the ability to accurately name how you feel.

I always planned on being a stay-at-home mom. The plan was to finish college, get married, get my master's degree, work my way up the corporate ladder then get pregnant with enough money saved to comfortably work from home or not at all. Well, *"A man makes his plans, but the Lord directs his steps."* (Proverbs 16:9) What actually happened was; I graduated college, got married, got pregnant, was put on bed rest and finished my master's degree the week before my oldest child was born. My executed plan was not organized. It was not seamless. It only roughly stuck to the bones of what I wanted. It was also exactly as God intended. At the very least I know God was not surprised.

I watched my friends' plans unfold much like mine. Their lives were unfolding similar to the plans they'd made, but not exactly and I began to let comparison set in. I'm sure you can relate we all do it at one time or another. We envy the couples who never seem to fight. The parents with the perfectly behaved children, the business men and women who seem to land accounts with ease and even the brother or sister in Christ who seem to have unwavering faith.

It is easy covet things when we only see one side, the side we don't have. We don't consider that the couple may have been through counseling to help them communicate effectively. Or that the parents spend so much time on discipline at home, that outside of the home there is little misbehavior. Nor do we hear the hundreds of "no's" the business man or women hear before landing a big account. Lastly, we have no idea how many hours of prayer and scripture reading, or how many situations requiring faith have occurred for that brother or sister to be so spiritually sound.

From time to time, I to, go through these moments of inadequacy from time to time. I get stuck in the trap of comparison and self-doubt. I start to wonder if I am being intentionally excluded or left out.

Sometimes I feel as if I am unworthy of companionship; after all what do I have to bring to the table? These are silent battles.

These battles are fought, lost and won within the confines of my mind. They rarely show up on the outside except in the case of desperate pleas for accountability and prayer. These are fights with whispers. Loud, persistent, haunting whispers in the dark. "You're not good enough." "You aren't successful enough." "You're not a good enough mom." "Your too hard." "You're too soft." "You. Are. Not. Enough."

Then there are the feelings that follow these whispers. Hopelessness, anger, fear... feelings are lies! They are fleeting vapors changing with circumstance or setting. I am not suggesting that feelings don't matter, they are very important, but they are rarely permanent, and they change quickly. The enemy loves to capitalize on our feelings. We use our feelings as excuses to make decisions both good and bad. We also use our feelings as a reason not to act. Our emotions should be more like advisors in our lives and less like dictators. Once we have identified how we allow our emotions to rule our lives, we can put them into their proper place.

While experiencing moments of inadequacy and comparison it is easy for me to transfer those feelings of frustration or irritation to my husband or children. It is easy to find scapegoat excuses, "Well, sure I am a little irritated, but they should have..." When justifications start, it is time for me to stop. It's time to pause and identify my true feelings and why. The Bible tells us it's important to know the affliction of our own hearts.

> **1 Kings 8:38 - 40** says, "If there is famine in the land, if there is pestilence, if there is blight or mildew, locust or grasshopper, if their enemy besieges them in the land of their cities, whatever plague, whatever sickness *there is,* [38] whatever prayer or supplication is made by any man or by all Your people Israel, each knowing the affliction of his own heart, and spreading his hands toward this house; [39] then hear in heaven Your dwelling place, and forgive and act and render

to each according to all his ways, whose heart You know, for You alone know the hearts of all the sons of men, **40** that they may fear You all the days that they live in the land which You have given to our fathers."

Life happens, hard times come, we lose people, money and things. Our heart gets broken, we experience hurt and sadness. This scripture is saying, whatever is going on in the world around you, know what is ailing you specifically. Then turn your attention to those in your family. Once you acknowledge and know how you truly feel you can come before the Lord knowing the root of the issue you want him to address.

> **Jeremiah 14:20** puts it this way, "We know our wickedness, O LORD, the iniquity of our fathers, for we have sinned against You."

I have come to realize when I am looking am focused on my inadequacies I am being self-centered. When I focus on what I am lacking, what desires are being unfulfilled and what areas may need work instead of focusing on God, what He has designed me to do, or getting closer to Him through studying His word, it becomes evident that the root of my issue is pride.

> *I have come to realize when I am looking am focused on my inadequacies I am being self-centered.*

I want to be as perfect as I can, so others will want me, want to be like me and see me as the correct example of Christ. I am not saying that we shouldn't address our issues and seek to be like Christ. We should wholly and completely surrender ourselves to be re-made by the creator of the universe. I am simply saying we need to constantly check our hearts, knowing our wickedness and acknowledging that if we were not wicked we wouldn't need Christ in the first place. My goal should not be that others see me as an example of Christ but that others see Christ only.

David says it so sincerely here,

> **Psalms 51:3** For I know my transgressions, And my sin is ever before me.

My heart translates this as, "I know I am not deserving of your love. In everything I do I see that." In verse 10 after acknowledging his state of being, he asks God, "Create in me a clean heart, O God, And renew a steadfast spirit within me."

David recognized that he was far from perfect; everywhere he looked he could see where he'd messed up. Yet this was the man that was after God's own heart. This man was a murderer, an adulterer, and a deserter; but he was also a warrior, a worshipper and a student of faith. He realized he did not deserve God's grace and he basked in it. David came to God as a child.

> **Matthew 18:3** "And said, Verily I say unto you, Except ye be converted, and become as little children, ye shall not enter into the kingdom of heaven."

My kids know there is nothing they can do to make me stop loving them. With this in mind they literally climb all over me at any given opportunity. They have no problem getting comfortable at the expenses of my discomfort. Even after getting in trouble they are right there by my side again, longing for my touch, for interaction with me. Sure they mess up, sure they have a lot to learn but they don't mind getting messy while learning.

David was like this. He made a mess of life at times, but he was steadfast and sure in God's love for him. He treated God like He was his father basking in His presence despite any previous infractions. This is how we should be with God. Sure that if nothing else is true, constant, and secure, His love is.

9

Another person who loved unapologetically was Peter. I just love Jesus' relationship with Peter. Peter was bold and daring and fiercely loved Jesus. Jesus walked alongside Simon Peter, a common fisherman. He befriended Peter and personally taught him the Word of God. Peter not only watched Jesus perform miracles he experienced them firsthand. Peter felt God's glory daily and was able to boldly say, He was the Son of God. Then, Peter denied he ever knew Jesus.

> **Luke 22:61** And the Lord turned and looked at Peter. Then Peter remembered the word of the Lord, how He had said to him, "Before the rooster crows,[h] you will deny Me three times." [62] So Peter went out and wept bitterly.

Peter was warned that He would deny Jesus. I don't think Jesus told Peter what would happen to make him feel bad but rather to forgive him in advance. When the rooster crowed, Peter was crushed. I imagine he was feeling embarrassed, sorry, and ashamed. Jesus hanging on the cross, looked right at him! What a weight! The story doesn't end there. God was going to remedy this situation.

> **Mark 16:12** says, "After that, He appeared in another form to two of them as they walked and went into the country."

As we read the same story from a different perspective in Luke 24:34, we find that one of those disciples was Peter. He could have appeared to any of the disciples. He eventually came to them all, but He came to Peter right away.

You may have felt like you've screwed up or you are not doing enough. Maybe you just aren't sure you are worth your weight in gold. Well let me tell you, Jesus did not overlook His friend who denied he knew Him while He was at His weakest, physically. You can rest assured that Jesus will not overlook you.

Peter learned, how we feel at the moment can quickly impact our decisions. When Peter told Jesus that he would not deny Him, I believe he was sincerely responding based on the emotions he felt at that time. He also denied Jesus based on his emotion at the crucifixion. Learning to identify your emotions is the first step of managing how those emotions manifest in our lives.

Knowing you were a sinner sentenced to death, to be saved only by God's grace and adopted as a co-heir with Christ, not only presents a testimony, but it reminds you where you came from. One Old Testament relationship I love is the relationship between Moses and Joshua. Moses choose Joshua for his skill as a warrior and recognized him apart from the other soldiers. Joshua was brave, strong, and steadfast. He soon had his own company to command and went to battle against the Amalekites.

As Joshua fought the Amalekites, the battle shifted and changed much like battles do. At some points, Joshua was winning. At other times, he was losing. Ultimately, Joshua and his soldiers won that battle. Joshua may have felt this was the normal progression of battle. As he was encouraging his soldiers on the physical battlefield he had no idea of what was happening in the spirit realm.

While Joshua was fighting, Moses was on top of a hill with Aaron and Hur. As long as Moses' hands were lifted, the Israelites would win the battle; as soon as his hands lowered, they began to lose. Ultimately Aaron and Hur had to help Moses by holding up his hands for him. There is no way Joshua could have been fully engaged in the battle he was fighting and continuously watching the hill where Moses stood. The only battle he was focused on was the physical one.

This is confirmed when we read, Exodus 17:14. God instructs Moses to tell Joshua all that was happening off the battlefield while he was fighting the Amalekites. Imagine Joshua learning that he did not win by his own might or skill, but by the power of God. The same happens in our daily lives.

There are spiritual battles that are happening as you fight your physical ones. Or you may be fighting a spiritual battle that you don't think you can win on your own. Let me encourage you not to try. That's right, do not try to battle on your own. The Bible encourages us to pray with others as there is power in touching and agreeing on the things you are praying over. After all, one can send a thousand demons to flight, two can send ten thousand! (Deut. 32:30) Your breakthrough may come through simply having another brother or sister in Christ there with you to hold up your hands when you no longer can.

As you are fighting life's battles, rest in the knowledge that God has a battle plan and He will be victorious. Imagine Joshua's surprise and awe at the knowledge that the position of Moses' hands directly correlated with his standing on the battlefield. If you are a Moses in someone's life, continue to hold up that banner. Pray continuously for their victory knowing that though they may not know now or ever recognize your role in the victory of that battle, it is fought and won for the glory of God.

An important part of self-awareness is knowing that you cannot do it alone. You were not *created* to do life alone. So as you are sorting through your feelings, connect with other believers through your local church and small groups.

> *An important part of self-awareness is knowing that you cannot do it alone.*

Developing self-awareness sometimes means talking out what your feeling until you can define how you are feeling. John 9:25 'He then answered, "Whether He is a sinner, I do not know; one thing I do know, that though I was blind, now I see."' It order to be emotionally intelligent one must recognize their own emotions FIRST. Once we get in the habit of recognizing and naming our emotions it makes it easier to assist others in identifying theirs.

"I hurt! I hurt! I hurt!" My two year old's screams echo through the house as she begs for a band aid to cover...a completely healed scar. She is doing this to put off nap time but it made me take a look at myself. See this is an old scar, from a self-inflicted wound, it's a small scar, but to her its huge especially when a challenge arrives. She immediately goes to a thing that hurt her in the past and reenacts those feelings rather than identifying her current feelings. She was two and did not have to vocabulary to express her desire to postpone bedtime. She did however remember how to hurt.

How many times have we screamed to God that we're hurting over a situation He has already healed? How many times do we use the excuse of past pain as a reason to act out of emotion rather than love. We yell, "I hurt! I hurt!" While God is prompting us to walk in our healing and serve as a light to the world. Scars serve as evidence of a past offense, but they could also serve as a reminder of God's grace and our overcoming a hurt. That place where the scar rests, is stronger and its mark serves as a badge of triumph. So, stop screaming it hurts, suck it up, get to the root of your emotions, name the feeling and use your words to pray it better. If you don't know the words to say, it's okay to say so. "God, I don't know how to express all that I am feeling but please search my heart and help me understand what I am feeling right now and how to respond to this situation the right way." I believe you can talk to God about anything! So, it is best to be transparent, there is absolutely nothing you can say to shock or surprise Him.

> *"God, I don't know how to express all that I am feeling but please search my heart and help me understand what I am feeling right now and how to respond to this situation the right way."*

Romans 5:3-5, "And not only that, but we also glory in tribulations, knowing that tribulation produces perseverance; and perseverance, character; and character, hope. Now hope does not disappoint, because the love of God has been poured out in our hearts by the Holy Spirit who was given to us."

We are going to go through hard times because it is good for us. Tribulations make us better because they build character and develop a dependence on God. He allows the scars to show us what it takes to develop our character. There are key situations in my life where people have hurt me, or situations have not gone as I'd desired, and I can tell you those wounds have provided priceless framework to building my character to what it is now. And what it will be.

I've had to look my hurt in the face and address it. Tear it apart. Examine it. Did hurt manifest because words spoken were true? Were they false? Was I dealing with hurt because I felt betrayed or because I put more faith in man than God? Was I in this situation because I was impatient and gave in to my immediate desires rather than focusing on my long-term goals? It can be difficult to tell the truth about yourself to yourself, but I have learned to practice emotional intelligence because it helps the wounds heal cleaner, faster, and with less scarring.

CHAPTER 2

How to Lead with Self Awareness

It is hard to be in church leadership. It seems there is always so much to be done, so many people to manage and different personalities to work with. With this in mind it's hard to gauge the condition of a church's self-awareness. Churches are made up of imperfect people and it is not feasible or appropriate to gauge the emotional intelligence of each member of your local church. So, you must look for clues and insight on the church's culture and the church leader's response to that culture.

> *In order to change the culture of your church you must first identify the aspects of your church culture that will hinder the success of your strategy.*

Business Guru Peter Drucker once said, "Culture eats strategy for breakfast." This is true in both corporations and the church. Let me explain. Maybe your vision is to grow your local church, to implement small groups or even to shift focus to your children's department. You may attend seminars and come up with an excellent strategy to change the dynamics at your church. However, if you do not also focus your efforts on changing the culture you will not be able to successfully implement your strategy. In order to change the culture of your church you must first identify the aspects of your church culture that will hinder the success of your strategy.

One way is to measure a church's Emotional Intelligence [EI] is by determining the excitement of its leaders. If the leaders are looking to include church members in leadership rather than protect church members from leadership or fellow members, this church is self-aware. It likely has leaders that display exemplary leadership qualities. Some qualities to look for and foster in your leaders are:

- Accountability
- Responsibility
- Dedication

Accountability

Let's look at accountability: Accountability and responsibility are listed as two separate elements because though they are similar in the secular world, in the church they take on a different dynamic. Accountability means you are doing what you have been assigned to do, and that those you report to are aware of it. In this case your church leaders should always be measuring themselves against the standard [Jesus]. Meaning they need to know what or rather who the standard is.

It is our responsibility to ask those under us how they are interacting with the Word of God daily. I am not suggesting they are questioned daily but rather they are questioned concerning their daily habits. This lets them know that what they do with God is more important than what they do for God.

> **Creating a culture of self-awareness through accountability, starts from the top down**

Creating a culture of self-awareness through accountability, starts from the top down. When leaders are held accountable it builds corporate moral by placing value on the task they are given. If you are asked to do something by a boss or manager and they never follow up or look for results you may be led to believe the task is not important to the end goal. If you are repeatedly questioned about the task in question, you are likely to complete it with a sense of urgency. If you are questioned about character traits that allow you to do the task well, you may be more likely to give your best.

For example: I ask my young adult leader to post about an upcoming event on social media and she agrees, then I never discuss it again. I do not go on social media and check for the posting. I do not mention to her that I did not hear any comments or reactions the post. I say absolutely nothing else about the matter. My young adult leader may or may not get around to completing the task but it is very likely she does not feel I value the task I have given her.

Example 2: I ask my young adult leader to post about an upcoming event on social media, and she agrees. I then began to call or send her a message every few hours questioning her progress. I check social media and grow frustrated when I don't see the message she agreed to conveyed. She is likely to feel that I have placed high value on this task. She is also likely to feel I have little trust in her to complete the task. So she may post something quickly just to stop me from asking.

> **Accountability is a quality that leads to self-awareness because it causes one to look at where they are honestly, in relation to where they are trying to go.**

Example 3: I ask my young adult leader to post about an upcoming event on social media, and she agrees. I tell her that I am confident in her diligence and expertise concerning the matter. I make clear my expectations and deadlines. I may call and offer my support and I may ask how close we are to meeting our deadline. She is likely to feel both invested in the task and aware of the high value I have placed on the task.

Accountability is a quality that leads to self-awareness because it causes one to look at where they are honestly, in relation to where they are trying to go.

Responsibility

Concerning responsibility. We must equip our leaders with authority while accurately explaining the weight of the responsibility they are taking on. We explain the weight of responsibility through demonstration. I learned trust and loyalty is easily gained through these three things. Praise in public, reprimand in private, and always taking the blame. If you do any work with me or for me, you can trust that I will make sure you are always viewed in a positive light.

I will take responsibility for tasks I have delegated missing deadlines or falling short and I will redirect praise for a job well done to my team or staff. This gives my team the security of knowing that working with me will help them succeed. My intent is always to leave a place better than when I arrived there.

Taking responsibility does not always mean taking the blame, though that will likely be required. Responsibility is completing the task, action or goal with a sense of complete ownership. Honesty is important when delegating responsibility. Years ago, my husband and I started attending a local church. Within our first year he was made Men's President. He didn't know what that entailed and when he asked, his oversight described a position that was far from the actual duties the position entailed. It was assumed that he had prior experience or understanding of how this church denomination and culture operated.

Unlike me, my husband did not grow up in a traditional brick and mortar church. His past experiences made him wary of church bureaucracy and politics. So being placed in a position that required he operate in both did not foster a positive view of the way that local church conducted their business.

He was not held accountable, he did not fully understand his responsibilities and that led to great frustration. He stepped down from that position, and it is now occupied by someone who feels called to and is thriving in this ministry.

> *By successfully identifying how they feel and why, leaders can pass on a sense of ownership to those working with them.*

Taking ownership of a task, project or ministry and successfully meeting previously set goals relies heavily on one's ability to self-assess. By successfully identifying how they feel and why, leaders can pass on a sense of ownership to those working with them. This will foster both loyalty to the cause and commitment to the goal.

Dedication

Lastly, a quality I would foster in my leaders is dedication. If you hold your leaders accountable, by caring more about their character than their task, and teach them responsibility by showing them clear pattern of behavior they can follow, they will show you true dedication. I will use my husband again as an example. He is one of the most dedicated people I know. While serving as a young leader at our local church he would work 40 plus hours a week, come home and play with our oldest daughter (the only child at the time), study the Word of God and go to church. He was accountable to our mentors, understood that his work with the church was an honor and responsibility as a believer and he gave his absolute best.

Our schedule at that time was crazy **incredibly busy**. Sunday mornings we **attended** church service. If we were serving that week, the rule was serve one, attend one. Tuesday evenings I had choir rehearsal. Wednesday evenings we served with the youth ministry. Thursday evenings we attended young adult service but did not serve. Every other Saturday we would drive 45 minutes away to meet with our Small Group. This seems like a lot as I am writing it, but it was never a burden, and we had so much fun!

The leaders we worked with were passionate, purpose-driven and filled with joy. They recognized the church wasn't perfect but didn't mind others seeing the imperfections because there was a plan in place to address the imperfections. The imperfections were to be addressed by new members coming in, utilizing their gifts and actively participating in the ministry. The church leaders communicated and operated as if God had already solved the problems. Not naïvely but expectantly.

One way to keep leaders excited is to help them identify how they feel about the current ministry in which they are serving. This does not mean that if they are unhappy with where they currently serving that they are in a place they shouldn't be. Rather by simply giving them a safe space to voice their feelings allows them to reframe their thoughts. Jeremiah, for example, had a life dedicated to sharing the heart of God with Israel and it was a far from easy task. Identifying how your leaders are feeling can help you get to the root of any covered or hidden issues as well as provide a sense of encouragement and relief. Issues left undiscovered may lead to bigger problems.

> *Proactive meetings are easier to conduct and have better outcomes than reactive meetings.*

Proactive meetings are easier to conduct and have better outcomes than reactive meetings. Instead of using your time convincing frustrated leaders to stay, meet with your leaders regularly and allow them a safe space to convey their feelings. It is better they share their frustrations with leaders above them than with congregants they are serving. This also creates a culture where leaders feel supported and heard.

To get a feel for the emotional intelligence of a church you can also look at the way the church responds to trends. There are some trends that can be helpful to the Body of Christ such as small groups, while others can be harmful such as twisting the Word of God to line up with the ideas and appetites of the world. The only measure to use is the Word of God. We will talk about motivation later on in this book, but the great commission should be behind the decisions made by your church leaders and the actions of the church should ALWAYS line up with the Word.

Church leaders are human, and while leading a ministry you have raised, a ministry you have cried and labored in, it is difficult to critically (or constructively) examine the ministry. Many church leaders recognize their weakness in this area and hire secret shoppers to visit their church services and give feedback. Hiring an outside perspective is a difficult, but sometimes necessary, step for church leaders to assess the true state of their church. Self-awareness in corporate form may mean acknowledging that as a leader you may not be able to objectively provide feedback.

One way to apply self-awareness practically to your local church, is to take the individual lessons on self-awareness and share it with church leaders in a way that is relevant to them personally as well as to their ministry. When leaders are intentional about equipping the leaders under them with techniques that grow them spiritually and emotionally those leaders are trained to respond to situations in an emotionally intelligent way.

Emotionally intelligent leaders have these key attributes in common. They complain up not down. These leaders understand that complaining down erodes confidence in the ministry; as well as how the ministry operates. Complaining up inspires solutions, often by the one with the complaint. This also sets precedent for congregants who follow in the culture set and exemplified by leadership.

Emotionally intelligent leaders can look at themselves honestly. If they don't have the skills or knowledge to do what is required of them they don't make excuses, they fill in the gaps. This may mean learning a new skill, leveraging the skills of those around them or recruiting someone who possess the skills they desire.

Emotionally intelligent leaders are not defensive. When dealing with conflict encourage your leaders to ask probing questions to identify if the problem is rooted in another issue. This teaches leaders to do the same when those under them are having trouble. Jesus showed the disciples how to handle conflict. It is in this spirit that we must lead. When you have a congregation full of self-aware leaders your church, by default will become more self-aware.

When having conversations due to conflict consider asking these questions to cause reflection:

How are you feeling?
Why do you feel this way?
What would you like to see happen?
How are you feeling?
What can I pray for?

It is human nature to want to defend those things that are important to us. However, I encourage you not to defend yourself or the ministry. Let the person you are counseling answer the questions asked, then respond to them as led by the Holy Spirit. A barrier to honest communication is the fear of hurting others' feelings. Asking questions allows you to help your leaders increase their self-awareness thus increasing their emotional intelligence.

CHAPTER 3

Self-regulation

Self-regulation is the ability to change one's emotions to encourage a desired outcome. Once we identify our emotions we can regulate those emotions to line up with the appropriate behavior for the environment. This can prove to be both difficult and eye opening. It can also leave people wondering what determines appropriate behavior. Having a standard of behavior for the environment you are in helps you translate your emotions into action.

When we respond to situations in our lives we should refer to the standard we adhere to. The word "standard", in this book, is defined as the governing set of rules for one's life. Standards can be set by our families, our culture, policies and procedures at work, laws or by our spiritual beliefs. There are times where these standards may overlap especially if your spiritual beliefs touch every area of your life. There may also be times where your standards conflict and put you in the position to prioritize them.

Self-regulation is an important next step in practicing Emotional Intelligence. After you know how you're feeling and why you're feeling that way it's easy to just stop there. It's easy to make an excuse as to why you said the things that you've said or exhibited the behavior that you did. However, to increase emotional intelligence, you must be willing to take the next step to regulate yourself.

Society and etiquette, which sets the cultural norms, often varies from place to place. Cultural norms set unspoken rules of interaction and sometimes these rules change according to the dynamic of the circumstance. One role of relationships in our lives is to assist us in navigating these changes. The believer's standard of appropriate behavior should always be the Word of God.

An example of a cultural norm is this: in some places women holding hands in public is a sign of friendship, but in that same culture those of the opposite sex holding hands in public may be frowned upon. Breaking the standard of appropriate behavior draws attention to the offender. I believe this is one reason we find comedy so amusing. It often takes the behavior we as a culture deem appropriate and turns it on its head.

Self-regulation can be like watching a train wreck happen in slow motion, except you have the ability to change its tracks, or even stop the crash. The faster you learn to identify your emotions, the faster you can regulate your response to feeling those emotions. This chapter will explore the importance of self-regulation as well as practical ways to implement it.

Have you ever met someone who could not control their facial expressions? They react to everything with their complete being. This is an example of a lack of emotional intelligence. These people may feel they are being genuine and transparent and they usually are. However, their expressions make it difficult for others to trust them or take them seriously.

People who react strongly are hard to share information with unless in a private setting. In a public environment they may draw attention with their expressions making it hard to share sensitive information. Their expressions show whether or not they agree with something before the speaker has finished speaking, making it difficult to take them seriously.

If you are an emotionally expressive person who is wondering how to increase emotional intelligence without betraying who you are, I encourage you to try this little trick. As a person is speaking to you, rather than react, repeat. Say every word they are saying to you inside your head. This will allow you to hear them completely while giving yourself the opportunity to regulate your emotions. In a business setting this will help you avoid offending others and while among friends this trick will help evoke a feeling of trust.

My days are full. I am a stay at home mom of three, I homeschool my children and I am a caretaker for my grandmother who is ill and is afflicted with Alzheimer's. My responsibilities often cause me to pause and look at my response habits. I find I get more and more frustrated on days that are long or extra full. After being with my family all day teaching, cooking, cleaning, rearing, praying and playing, I am exhausted.

Some days are filled with meetings, doctor's appointments, phone calls and church business. Other days are filled with relaxation and family time. Recognizing this, I realized it isn't fair for me to yell or react out of irritation as the day goes on. After all, the behavior of my family hadn't really changed much from the beginning of the day to the end of the day. It was my perspective that had changed as my disposition was altered by exhaustion.

Taking more time to respond as the day goes on allows me to exercise grace. I have also learned not everything needs to be done immediately. I can get so busy that I miss important moments. For example, l eat a different diet than the rest of my family, so I make their meals first. Unfortunately, by the time I sit down to eat, they are finished. I end up cleaning and eating later. Lately, I have been intentional about sitting down with my children for dinner. I know that one day they will have families of their own, so these days of eating with them as small children are numbered.

I've learned through the years that my words hold immense power. Recognizing that my frustration grows with the day makes me take more time to pause and be still. I don't want to say something out of frustration or anger that will negatively shape the way my children move through the world. My cousin came to visit and asked how I was so calm after a bedtime filled with tantrums and screaming from my one year old. I told her I parent as if I have an audience.

> **I parent as if I have an audience, because I do!**

I try to treat my children as if they are on loan to me. In the beautiful said words of my friend, "We are but stewards of the gifts bestowed upon us by Jesus." I am babysitting for God. The thing is, He is right there watching me with His children. I parent as if I have an audience, because I do! I have also learned children repeat everything, even our behaviors. When my children practice parenting on their toys and dolls I hear how I speak to them echoed by them.

Faith comes by hearing (Romans 10:17). Psalm 33:6 remind us that God created the universe with His words. Genesis 1:27 says we were created in the image of God. If my kids hear what I say, they will believe what I say. If my kids say what I say they will see what they say. I want the manifestation of words in their life to be a beautiful masterpiece of God's love and grace.

I want them to hear mommy saying, "Love is patient." Then repeat it. I want to hear them say, "Be generous and willing to share." (1 Timothy 6:18) I want them to speak the Word of God over their lives. Those words have power. Those words create universes.

I've also learned that during times of stress, emotions run high. It is in this place, I must base my actions on fact rather than feeling. In 2014 my grandmother was taken to the emergency room for a sore back. We discovered she had stage 4 metastatic breast cancer. The doctor said her body was a train wreck. My grandmother is well loved, so this news was devastating.

I couldn't cry. I couldn't accept that this hospital was the end of the line for her. I simply began to ask questions. I needed to know as many details as possible. I didn't know if this would save her life or not, but I had to try. I had to know that I tried. I wasn't sure if my positive words would make it better, but I knew that negative ones would make it worse.

I took the information, the details I received from the doctor and I prayed. I prayed specific prayers based on the information I gathered. My family rallied around my grandmother and covered her with love, knowing this situation was in God's hands and that he had the final say. After being given 6 months to live by the doctors she has gone on to live years, she is currently not only alive, but thriving!

One of my favorite stories in the Bible about the power of words is the story of Zechariah and Elizabeth in the first chapter of Luke. Zechariah was told by an angel of the Lord, he and Elizabeth would have a child. This was a surprise because Elizabeth was older in age. Zechariah did not understand how this could be, so he questioned God. As a result, he was struck dumb until his son's birth. He could not verbally share his opinion on anything during his wife's entire pregnancy.

Sometimes the plan God has for us is so beyond us that we question its validity. We want to react out of feeling rather than pausing and lining our feeling up to the standard we have placed in our lives. God has laid out a purpose that is impossible to complete without him. When I read this story, I thank God for His mercy.

Rather than take away Zechariah's son and give the gift of his parenthood to another couple He took away Zechariah's ability to compromise that gift or the circumstances surrounding it. He regulated Zechariah's emotions and when we are filled with the Holy Spirit, God will regulate our emotions. If you have a hard time controlling how you feel there is no need to stress or worry, surrender to the creator of the universe. He will guard His word concerning you.

Proverbs 18:21 "Death and life are in the power of the tongue: and they that love it shall eat the fruit thereof." Our words are vital and once spoken they cannot be taken back. Their initial sting cannot be replaced and the damage they evoke can rarely be completely repaired. This makes self-regulation vital to the health of our personal relationships.

Proverbs 4:23 says, "Above all else guard your heart for it is the wellspring of life."

When we are mindful of the things we allow in our hearts we can have greater control of what comes out of our mouths.

Luke 6:45 says, "A good man out of the good treasure of his heart bringeth forth that which is good; and an evil man out of the evil treasure of his heart bringeth forth that which is evil: for of the abundance of the heart his mouth speaketh."

If we only allow good things to enter our hearts, we are less likely to speak damaging things to ourselves or others. We can protect our hearts by monitoring what we are seeing and hearing. Once we see something we cannot un-see it and once we hear something we cannot control the effect is has on our psyche. This is why audio cues are a big component of brainwashing. When we are vigilant about what we allow in our hearts our emotions are easier to identify thus easier to regulate.

Years ago I was swept up in a craze. There was a very popular show on TV, where the main character was sleeping with a married man. The writing was interesting, the characters engaging but the focus of the show was this woman and her romanticized relationship with this married man. As I watched the show it is hard not to root for the success of this couple.

I sat riveted as I watched the actress who played the wife of the man cry and fight for her failing marriage and I was entertained. My mother stopped me one day as I was re-capping the latest episode for her and asked, "How can you as a woman, a wife and believer be entertained by something that goes against everything you believe?" Woah! That stopped me in my tracks and I never watched another episode. Self-regulation may mean giving up what the culture deems appropriate to follow what the Word of God says to do. This may mean giving up things we enjoy.

> **Philippians 4:8** says, "⁸ Finally, brethren, whatsoever things are true, whatsoever things are honest, whatsoever things are just, whatsoever things are pure, whatsoever things are lovely, whatsoever things are of good report; if there be any virtue, and if there be any praise, think on these things." If what you are putting in does not line up with this verse it needs to be re-examined.

Self-regulation helps you develop a life of honesty and integrity. When you have a standard that you measure yourself against, you are less likely to stray from your goals. One of the sayings in our house is, "We finish what we start." My kids are quick to remind me of this when I get frustrated with a deadline I am trying to meet, if they hear me contemplating ending a project or assignment early.

> *When you have a standard that you measure yourself against, you are less likely to stray from your goals.*

Self-regulation also helps establish clear boundaries. The Word of God serves as the standard for my life. The Word outlines clear do's and don'ts for my life and following them means setting boundaries. Boundaries are important because they are not just for keeping people out but for protecting what is within them. I use boundaries to protect my family and our legacy.

For example, as a follower of Christ it is my responsibility to take time to spend with God. I must also be an example to my children as I raise them in the way they should go. I have a responsibility to my family and the legacy we are leaving to be a good steward of our time, talents and resources. As a result, I do not accept calls concerning work for the church before noon unless the kids are on break. I limit phone conversations after 6pm when my husband is home so I can spend quality time with him. I also protect our family time on Saturdays by making arrangements for my grandmother's care when necessary.

Boundaries bring about security. My family has no doubt that after God they are the priority in my life. Through them seeing and testing my dedication, I pray they see the love of God.

> **Proverbs 13:3** says, "Those who guard their lips preserve their lives, but those who speak rashly will come to ruin."

Self-regulation is simply taking your emotions and measuring them against the standard in your life. In the story of Zechariah his inability to speak was the ultimate blessing; because it meant he could not speak against his son's destiny. Imagine if he had retained the ability to speak. I'm sure the story would have been quite different. He may have placed doubt in his wife's heart with his words. Those words would have come with consequences. Those consequences would have re-shaped the story.

I am still writing my story. Therefore, I know that as my day goes on, I need to regulate my behavior. To help me measure myself against the standard I decided to practice, *"the pause."* When I am feeling frustrated rather than react or respond... I pause. For example, when my kids start fighting, instead of yelling out of frustration or sending them to bed, I pause. I look at why they're fighting, how they're feeling and let's keep it real, I look at the clock to see how close we are to bedtime.

After I assess the situation, I respond. Sometimes the response of fussing and telling them to get ready for bed is warranted. Other times one of them may have a valid concern that needs to be addressed. Either way, I know in order to be an emotionally intelligent parent and most importantly for my kids to see God's love through me, I must pause as the day goes on. I admit I also must apologize from time to time as well. I find that the best leaders take the blame and deflect the praise. They also admit when they are wrong. Many times, self-regulation looks like humility.

Honesty is as important to self-regulation as it is to self-awareness. I am honest with myself and at least one other person about how I feel when faced with tough situations. I'm an honest person in general but I tend to be very private about my personal feelings. So, I share unfiltered thoughts with either my husband, my mother or my sister. I usually have to talk through how I feel, so I do it with someone that allows me to backtrack and over-explain, all while asking probing questions.

> **Ephesians 4:25** Therefore, putting away lying, "Let each one of you speak truth with his neighbor,"[a] for we are members of one another.

In the spirit of the scripture above I am going to share with you a very popular passage of scripture that we often hear read at weddings. If you come to my house on a loud, busy day when the kids seem to prefer me disheveled you will hear me mumbling it under my breath.

> 1 **Corinthians 13:4-13** "Love is patient, love is kind. It does not envy, it does not boast, it is not proud. **5** It does not dishonor others, it is not self-seeking, it is not easily angered, it keeps no record of wrongs. **6** Love does not delight in evil but rejoices with the truth. **7** It always protects, always trusts, always hopes, always perseveres. **8** Love never fails. But where there are prophecies, they will cease; where there are tongues, they will be stilled; where there is knowledge, it will pass away. **9** For we know in part and we prophesy in part, **10** but when completeness comes, what is in part disappears. **11** When I was a child, I talked like a child, I thought like a child, I reasoned like a child. When I became a man, I put the ways of childhood behind me. **12** For now we see only a reflection as

in a mirror; then we shall see face to face. Now I know in part; then I shall know fully, even as I am fully known. [13] And now these three remain: faith, hope and love. But the greatest of these is love."

You won't hear the whole passage come from my lips, but you may catch me saying, "Love is patient, love is patient, love IS patient." When my days are hard, and my children seem to have sleeping ears. You may even catch me mumbling, "Love never fails." This passage of scripture is an anthem of motherhood for me. As I grow I have learned to embrace the standard the Word of God continues to set for my life.

Self-regulation is a part of spiritual growth. It is not something we arrive at but rather something we continue to grow into. Verse 11 of 1 Corinthians 13 refers to thinking as a child. A child has issues regulating their emotions. Children do not have the vocabulary or maturity to express how they feel. The way they feel is often too big to measure against a standard which is why they have parents and mentors to teach them how to appropriately decode and express those feelings.

Self-Regulation can mean accepting your own humanity and forgiving yourself. I have made decisions that I wish I hadn't. Maybe I should have made that choice, maybe I shouldn't. Either way, I must forgive myself realizing I made the best choice I could at the time.

> **Romans 8:1** There is therefore now no condemnation to those who are in Christ Jesus,[a] who do not walk according to the flesh, but according to the Spirit.

> *God is not surprised by our actions and He always keeps a door back to Him, wide open.*

There is no condemnation in Christ Jesus! God is not surprised by our actions and He always keeps a door back to Him, wide open.

Forgiveness does not mean without consequence. There are natural consequences to our actions and we should handle them with grace. Sometimes those consequences are broken relationships, costly fines or even loss of status or property. When God forgives an imprisoned criminal, his sentence is not revoked but the peace of God may be the only thing that carries the criminal to the sentence's completion.

> **Matthew 5:29-30** If your right eye causes you to sin, tear it out and throw it away. For it is better that you lose one of your members than that your whole body is thrown into hell. And if your right hand causes you to sin, cut it off and throw it away. For it is better that you lose one of your members than that your whole body goes into hell.

We must cut the bad habits out of our lives, so our lives don't end up in ruin. Since we can't fix it all we must accept that some things are simply out of our control.

> **Romans 8:28** And we know that all things work together for good to them that love God, to them who are the called according to his purpose.

We must also resolve that ultimately things are working out for our benefit. Even as we face hardships. Our feelings are seen and understood by God.

It is important we change our focus from that of self-pity to one of gratitude. It is for this reason my family takes professional pictures every year. We have a great photographer that scouts a location, styles the family and bribes the kids so we get big genuine smiles. It's an investment in my marriage and in my family.

It is hard to be upset with my husband when I am looking at his handsome face all over the house. I can't hold a grudge when I see the way he is looking at me in the pictures I keep in my planner. It also helps me remember to pray over what we have. We want to leave a legacy of love for generations to follow.

It's hard to wish my kids would hurry up and pass a developmental milestone when I am looking at their changing faces grow and develop. They grow up so fast and every year their little faces change. Parenthood truly is long days and short years. Children seeing themselves happy in pictures also builds their confidence and self-esteem. They began to see themselves as beautiful. *1 Thessalonians 5:18 In* everything *give thanks, for this is the will of God in Christ Jesus concerning you.*

It is important to note that self-regulation does not always mean taking the most pleasant or placid road. It is responding appropriately for the situation. The military has many great examples of self-regulation. In this facet of our society, emotional intelligence can be the very thing that keeps soldiers alive.

It is completely appropriate for a Drill Sergeant to yell orders to a private during basic training. It would not be expected or even recommended that they speak in low, calm, peaceful tones. The urgency in the sergeant's voice invokes immediate obedience. This may be the difference between life and death on the battlefield.

In basic training the standard is set. Sergeants are to speak in a tone and volume that invokes immediate reaction because that is the most appropriate for their position. Soldiers must obey and act. It would be inappropriate and dangerous for a soldier to burst into tears on the battlefield because his Sergeant spoke harshly.

The same can be said for our children. We should raise them with love and gentleness but there are situations that occur where it is necessary for parents to respond to a child's behavior with sternness and strength. Discipline is an important aspect of parenting and parents approach it many ways. The most important thing is children understanding boundaries that keep themselves and others safe from harm.

My parents say they were hardest on us when we were younger. There were a lot of tantrums and frustrated cries, but as we grew they we able to use logic and reason to communicate with us. My parents understood that we could not comprehend the vocabulary necessary for compliance at 1 year old. Using self-regulation they learned to discipline us in a way that protected us while letting us be children.

You should always be the hardest person on you. When you look for ways to correct yourself and to better line up with the Word of God, the correction and accountability from other people is less frustrating. If every time someone offers you correction you get frustrated or irritated that is an indication that you either do not have a standard that you are measuring yourself up against or your standard is you. Both of those conditions are outside of the will of God.

To regulate yourself, start small. Set measurable goals and set yourself up to win. You want to deal with the root of the problem you uncovered in the self-awareness stage of thinking. Then you address the symptoms of that problem. For example, if your problem is that you believe you are the standard. Then a measurable goal that allows you to regulate yourself may be to establish a standard in your life. I use the Bible as my standard because it is true, unchanging and it requires a response for my belief.

Your standard should be unchanging and unwavering. When you measure yourself against it, it should be unbiased. If your root issue is the lack of a standard, but you desire to live by The Word of God, one idea for a win would be for the next 5 days to read the Bible every time you pick up your phone. To win you can read the same verse multiple times a day or you can read versus in succession for the next 5 days. You could even read a chapter of the Bible a day for the next 5 days.

Only you know what a measurable goal that you can win is. After the 5 days is up you have accomplished your goal, you're feeling good about yourself, you've regulated your behavior. Reading the Word of God everyday has changed your disposition. You feel better about yourself because in this 5-day routine you've measured up by getting closer to the standard you set, than you were on day one.

Congratulations, you are now closer to the standard that you were on day one!

Now you set your next goal. You may choose for the next 5 days to do a devotion or go on a prayer walk or perhaps get up 30 minutes earlier to meditate on the Word of God. You want your next goal to be a little bit more challenging than the first goal. With the first goal you set yourself up to win. You've established that you can keep your word to yourself. You use that established behavior to establish behavior.

Once you've uncovered the root of those issues and you've addressed the root of your issues through setting goals and accomplishing those goals your emotional intelligence will begin to increase.

CHAPTER 4

How to Lead with Self-Regulation

Corporate self-regulation is something the church is good at. The whole purpose of the church is to learn steps to regulate our emotions and draw closer to God. We then go out and invite others to accept the Word of God as the standard by which they regulate their lives.

It is vital to the spiritual health of a church to teach holy and righteous living. If congregants are actively reading their Bible and praying consistently, the by product of their actions will be evident in their life.

> **Galatians 5:22-23** But the fruit of the Spirit is love, joy, peace, longsuffering, kindness, goodness, faithfulness, [23] gentleness, self-control. Against such there is no law.

It is difficult to pray without ceasing and be in a bad mood. If you are constantly seeking the will of God through prayer and Bible reading you will operate in love, you will have joy, you will be at peace, you will demonstrate patience, kindness, goodness and faithfulness.

All too often, church leaders become so busy doing the work of the church that they neglect their personal relationship with God. This may leave them feeling frustrated and defeated when things don't go their way rather than feeling encouraged and resting in the fact that God is not surprised. It can become easy to overlook the little things like corporate prayer in the church office before starting the day or checking in with church leaders concerning their personal devotion time.

These little foxes destroy the vine (Song of Solomon 2:15). They lead to bigger issues and these bigger issues lead to bigger issues. It can be difficult to identify where the initial problem lies but we can rest assured in our awesome God. Little habits can be the thing that restores life into the local church. Things like group prayer and devotion can have a huge impact on the spiritual strength of the local church.

I am referring to an atmosphere where everyone is sharing their hearts, not listening to a sermon or pastor led Bible study. Sermons and Bible Studies have their place, but they do not elicit an immediate response. When addressing issues that require confession and communication, such as lack of accountability, accountability, this is best obtained in a small group setting.

When leaders are not held accountable it becomes easy for their spiritual health to be overlooked. It is easy for leaders to look physically sound by doing church culture things. They may raise their hands during worship, pray loud and strong, they may even have the loudest, "Amen" as the sermon is delivered. Church leaders and seasoned church members know how to say the right things and how to make recognizing spiritual jaundice very difficult. This can be remedied by setting up structures within the church to encourage growth through discipleship and accountability.

I recently conducted a survey at a church leaders meeting about the prayer are Bible reading habits of the leaders. These leaders were faces you would see Sunday morning and for mid-week services. My survey focused on their alone time with God. The results showed that 90% of the church leaders would pray and read their Bible more often IF they were held accountable. When leaders are working together to accomplish the goals they have set in the self-awareness stage, they are more likely to achieve their goals because they want to have a favorable answer for the people asking.

It is important that church members and leaders understand that though they can't "act" their way saved, the world should see transformation in their lives because of the infilling of the Holy Spirit. Act 2:38 says, "Then Peter said to them, "Repent, and let every one of you be baptized in the name of Jesus Christ for the remission of sins; and you shall receive the gift of the Holy Spirit.""

In Acts chapter two the multitude that heard Peter speak was not simply moved by seeing the believers speak in tongues but by the Prophecy that was spoken by Joel.

> **Acts 2:15 - 17** "For these are not drunk, as you suppose, since it is *only* the third hour of the day.
>
> [16] But this is what was spoken by the prophet Joel:
>
> [17] 'And it shall come to pass in the last days, says God, That I will pour out of My Spirit on all flesh; Your sons and your daughters shall prophesy, Your young men shall see visions, Your old men shall dream dreams.
>
> [18] And on My menservants and on My maidservants I will pour out My Spirit in those days; And they shall prophesy.
>
> [19] I will show wonders in heaven above And signs in the earth beneath: Blood and fire and vapor of smoke.
>
> [20] The sun shall be turned into darkness, And the moon into blood, Before the coming of the great and awesome day of the LORD.
>
> [21] And it shall come to pass *That* whoever calls on the name of the LORD Shall be saved."

Peter was clear that the gift of the Holy Spirit was more about what God would reveal to the receiver than what the receiver would show the world. If your leaders are quick to show their spiritual gifts but slow to spend time with God to discover the treasures of His heart hidden in His word, they need a fruit check.

I don't believe the Pharisees ever intended to miss the Savior. They were so used to "doing church" that they didn't understand how to "be" the church. Now, even though we have the resources the Pharisees didn't, it is easy to fall into the same practice. Acting the part becomes more important than being who God is asking us to be. The change is easy. All it requires is time with Him.

We put more time, money, and energy in maintaining church buildings than we do on the streets where the broken people are. We use Luke 14:23 as an excuse to hide in our buildings and beckon unbelievers to come to a building to meet Jesus. However, when we are filled with the Holy Ghost we become the church. Let's examine that scripture.

Jesus tells the story of a great feast. This feast was prepared for specific guests who for one reason or another could not come.

> **Luke 14:23**, "And the lord said unto the servant, Go out into the highways and hedges, and compel them to come in, that my house may be filled."

> **1 Corinthians 3:16** "Know ye not that ye are the temple of God, and that the Spirit of God dwelleth in you?"

We are the temple of God when we are compelling people to come. We are compelling them to hear what we are saying. The feast is within us and we have more than enough to give.

Imagine if every church shut its doors and had services, in parks or public places just like Jesus. How many people would walk up off the street to see and hear this great spectacle. It would be less about numbers and reaching budget goals and more about seeing lives change before our eyes. There are ministers all over the world doing this even now. Leaving their comfortable churches and choosing instead to "rough it" by doing street ministry.

We live in a time of information; people know what we believe. They can read a Bible or hear a sermon online what they want to see. What will convert unbelievers is life change. This is done through relationships. It's done through doing ministry the way Jesus did.

Small Groups, Life Teams, or even Home Bible Studies serve as a vehicle for accountability and discipleship. When a small group of people get together to learn about living out the Word of God, they form a community which in turn strengthens the faith of everyone in the group. This group uses self-regulation and becomes more like God. Simply put, the more time you spend with God the more you look like Him.

> **Jesus led a small group.**

Jesus led a small group. He taught thousands, but he discipled 12. His small group went with Him almost everywhere He went. He was dedicated to teaching His group what He knew and giving them room to flourish. I love how Jesus sent His disciples out to perform miracles and preach about the kingdom of God in Luke 9. Discipleship is about equipping members of the body of Christ to move forward in their walk. There should be measurable spiritual progress.

As leaders we must empower those we work with to do the things God has placed in them to do. In order to effectively do this, we must know them, their goals and what they feel their calling is. Jesus knew the disciples and those who would become believers long before He came to earth to save us. Yet, He still took the time to form relationships with His disciples. We must connect with each other for the purpose of furthering the kingdom of God through the activation of our purpose.

Following the example of Christ, the modern church was born through Home Bible Studies. The book of Acts laid out the entire process. The church grew and developed through groups of people getting together and studying scripture. It was in these home groups that the Word of God was dissected and explained.

Leaders should be in a position where they are expected to lead as well as be a part of a small bible study or disciple group. Being in a group with peers will ensure their spiritual needs are addressed so they will be better equipped to lead others. Too often leaders fall into a life of sin or mentorship outside of the church, because they are not a part of a group of spiritual peers that can and will hold them accountable. This sin may not be as obvious as infidelity or drug use it may be as simple as not doing something God told them to do or not responding to their convictions.

The suicide rate for ministers and pastors is heartbreaking. By setting up accountability habits early in a ministry and discussing these habits from the pulpit or stage, pastors can teach their leaders how to protect themselves from physical and spiritual attacks.

It breaks my heart when leaders fall into situations that result in divorce. Sometimes leaders can be so opposed to correction that they only receive it from those of a certain status. This is not only prideful but unfortunate. The Word of God lets us know through the examples of both Samuel and Timothy that physical age does not qualify or absolve someone from hearing and acting on the Word of God.

Eli served in the temple as a priest for many decades before Samuel came along. He was priest long before Samuel was born. It was through Eli's lips that a word was spoken over Hannah followed by Samuel's conception and birth. Eli has status, and it is evident that he hears from God. So when we look at Samuel chapter 3, we need to understand that there is a reason God choose to speak to Samuel. He wasn't just sending a message to Eli, He was sending a message to us all.

His message to Eli, in short, was: everything I told you I would do concerning your family I will do. I believe God was reminding Eli that the experience of hearing His voice was a privilege. At that time, it was uncommon for God to appear before man if they were not priests, which makes the various accounts we see in the Bible so priceless. We do not know exactly how long it took for Samuel to become a priest after his conversation with Eli, but we do know the mantel was passed down.

In the story of Eli and Samuel we also learn another important lesson. Your mentee will and should succeed you. Eli taught Samuel how to recognize the voice of God and Samuel's obedience resulted in an unfavorable message to Eli. When you train your leaders, you are not training them to be loyal to you, you are training them to be loyal to God even if that means calling you out if necessary.

> *Your mentee will and should succeed you.*

This story also shows us that leadership does not absolve us of the responsibilities to our family. God's words to Eli were, "Behold, I will do something in Israel at which both ears of everyone who hears it will tingle. [12] In that day I will perform against Eli all that I have spoken concerning his house, from beginning to end. [13] For I have told him that I will judge his house forever for the iniquity which he knows, because his sons made themselves vile, and he did not restrain them. [14] And therefore I have sworn to the house of Eli that the iniquity of Eli's house shall not be atoned for by sacrifice or offering forever." (1 Samuel 3:11)

Eli was busy doing the work of the Lord, but he did not watch out for his sons' spiritual health. At this time in history the priesthood was often passed down from father to son. I have seen it time and time again Pastors and Ministers so committed, so dedicated to their ministries that they've lost the ability to spiritually influence their children. I've seen leaders put the church before their families and that destroys their ability to minister to their families. God equipped Eli to be able to be both priest and parent. Eli used his duties as priest to negate his duties as a parent.

Having strong relationships with your children can also serve the ministry well. When your children are involved with and excited about what you are doing for God they are more likely to continue serving in the church as adults. When I have an issue as a parent I am not going to talk to someone who is struggling in the same area no matter what their credentials say. I am going to talk to someone who has children who love the Lord and are serving in the ministry.

When our kids are spiritually cared for it shows the world that what we believe is not a set of rules and statutes. It is not simply tradition and exhortation. It is a relationship with God that teaches us to move in a way that blesses others and furthers the gospel of Jesus Christ.

If you are not used to communicating with your leaders except to instruct or reprimand, conversing for the sake of assessing their spiritual health can be daunting for both parties. One way to start these crucial conversations is by asking open-ended questions about their relationship with God.

Here are some examples:

Are you reading the Bible daily? (If not, what hurdles are making this difficult.)

What is God talking to you about through His word? (They should always be measuring themselves against the standard.)

Are there any conflicts you are facing in your group that you need to discuss?

CHAPTER 5

Motivation

Our motivation is the reason behind our actions. We are often motivated by external forces that trigger our emotions, causing an action as a response. Some motivations are simple. We eat, because we are hungry. Others are complex, we lash out because we feel defensive, as a result of a past hurt. Examining the motivation for actions, forces us to face our shortcomings and measure them against the standard.

As a parent I struggle with this aspect of emotional intelligence the most often. Did I raise my voice to my children because they needed to hear the volume increase in order to heed my instructions or was it because I was tired or bothered by something else? With this in mind, I've decided to give my children more grace as the day goes on. I also, intentionally, express my feelings to my children. I say things like, "Mommy is tired, mommy is frustrated, even mommy is sad." Sharing my feelings with them equips them with the proper vocabulary to express their feelings and to be aware of the differences between them. This also gives them a model by which to express their feelings, teaching them self-awareness by example.

The practice of putting words to my feelings also allows me to effectively identify and acknowledge my motivation. When I acknowledge the motivation behind my action, I take accountability. It is human nature and immature to deflect the blame for both our feelings and actions. These things are controlled by us. My mother uses the term "hurt feelings switch." She would ask who flipped my hurt feelings switch. She would also remind me that I can switch it off at any time. Accepting responsibility has helped me quickly overcome any issue I faced.

Motivation is a slippery thing. It seems to come in droves when a major life event occurs such as a birth, marriage, birthday, death or even the beginning of a new year. We say things like, "I am motivated to do things differently now." Motivation also seems to be attached to things that go against our nature. Self-discipline seems to outweigh comfort and meeting goals seems more important than maintaining the status quo. With time that motivation wanes and old habits return.

The same can be said when it comes to our emotional responses to things. There is a peak in the day where we have hit our stride. We face the world ready to take on our task with confidence. We may be motivated by a sense of accomplishment, or the need to produce. Whatever the reason, our outcomes are a result of our internal drive. Our motivation.

The use of cutting words during an argument may be the most common example of the importance of addressing our motivators. Everyone at one point or another has said things, that are not relevant to the conflict they are having at the time. Rather than focus on the subject at hand, we may instead decided to personally attack our opponent. The most obvious motivation for these things is to cause pain. We don't like to admit that we use our words or actions with the intent to cause damage, so we usually justify this action with another motivation. Especially, when there is no threat of actual physical harm.

The person using words in a cutting manner does so to establish a sense of authority, to overpower the person they're attacking. We don't like to use words like "attacking" when referring to hurtful things said in the argument. However, if you look at the motivation behind cutting words the intent is often, at its simplest, to get someone to do what you want them to do. This behavior is often done from a position of wanting to be superior.

When we are self-aware, we recognize that we have a problem, we recognize that we feel a certain way, and we put words to our feelings to explain them to ourselves and others. Motivation makes you really examine your feelings and establish why you have allowed those feelings to manifest into action. In the self-regulation phase, it is possible to alter one's actions before they are acted upon. We can regulate how we are feeling by analyzing our environment then determining the best outcome for the occasion.

> *Emotional intelligence is a decision, that becomes a habit, that becomes a character trait.*

If we can regulate our feelings, then we can alter our motivation. emotional intelligence is a practice. It is a way of being. It is going through the phases so often that it becomes seemingly second nature. Emotional intelligence is a decision, that becomes a habit, that becomes a character trait.

Motivation may be the most important part of emotional intelligence. It is a vital part of the human experience. We eat because we are motivated by our stomachs and by our displeasure towards discomfort. We are motivated to work so that we can eat and so that those we love can eat. We are motivated by stressors to defend ourselves or run away.

A part of emotional intelligence is realizing that we have control over the things that motivate us. We build our lives through our decisions. Life is not happening to us, we are creating the life that we want to live around us. A huge part of internal motivation is personal responsibility. It's taking responsibility for where we are in the moment, and why we are where we are in the moment. We must stop and ask ourselves, "What is motivating this decision?"

Our motivation, as Christians should always be love. We are commanded to love God with all our being, then to love others as ourselves. (Luke 10:27) I've always found this scripture to be striking. We need to be instructed to love God with everything in us, because that is not our nature. Our nature is to love ourselves more than anything. Once we regulate our motivation, we are instructed to put ourselves on the same level as our neighbors.

It is difficult to love people in this way. This requires a constant check against the standard. This requires a constant check of motivation. Once we identify what has been motivating us and we identify what we feel should be motivating us, we can take the steps necessary to foster and grow the motivators that we want to direct our lives.

For example, I love my children, I want my children to be happy, I want my children to be smart and more than anything I want my children to live their respective purposes. I want my children to have the freedom to explore their ideas and discover the world around them through their very unique eyes. This is the motivation behind me homeschooling my children. This is my "why", so to speak.

This purpose is why I am motivated to get up early in the morning and make sure they have a hot breakfast on most days. This purpose is why I am motivated to sit up late at night, getting materials together for different activities and crafts that we will be doing throughout the week. This purpose is what motivates me to read and study how their little brains work and how to best convey information to them. My motivation is my love for my children and my desire to see them fulfill their God-given purposes.

It is also possible to be motivated by what we don't want to happen. This kind of motivation has changed my diet, the way I discipline my children and it even shapes the way I speak to my husband. I don't want to get cancer or diabetes or Alzheimer's. These are diseases that have touched my family. I do not know if my choices will prevent them but I do my best to avoid activities that I know may assist them in destroying my body. I don't want a relationship with my children where they can't talk me. I want my children to experience unconditional love from me. I don't want a relationship where they have to wonder if my behavior towards them is dictated by my fleeting emotions. I don't want a relationship where my husband feels he has to hide things from me or where we cannot be a safe place for one another.

Please understand that these things are not rooted in fear, they are rooted in information. I understand that life and death is in the power of the tongue and I don't want to kill my relationships with my words. I have seen relationships where the wife cannot trust her husband. I have seen relationships where the children cannot talk to their parents. I have seen people with horrible diets contract diseases. In order to change your motivation, you have to be self-aware and practice self-regulation.

Every component of emotional intelligence ties together as if it were a braid or a woven tapestry. It's important to understand that you can't have one part of emotional intelligence and ignore the rest. In order to effectively identify and change your motivations, you must first identify how you feel and where you currently are. That is self-awareness. Knowing what motivates you and using that to reach your end goal is self-regulation. Deciding to account for the feelings of others, brings in the empathy and relationship components of emotional intelligence. These things work together to help you better respond to the world around you and ultimately reach your desired outcomes.

If you don't have an angle, purpose or thing that is pushing you, that is driving you to do your best, then your motivation is not going to be strong enough to propel you into the kind of life that you desire. Your motivation should push you along, it should not be something you pull along. For example, you may wish your motivation was love, when it is really fame. This will put you into position to pretend you are operating in love when you really are not. This is exhausting and eventually your true colors show.

When your motivation is not clear, spend more time with God. Psalm 37:4 tells us that if we delight in the Lord, He will give us our heart's desires. You may be frustrated wondering if this scripture is true. Maybe you are waiting for that promotion or financial increase. Maybe you are waiting for that spouse or maybe you are waiting for children. This scripture is still true. The more time you spend with God, the more your desires change to look more like His desires.

> **When your motivation is not clear, spend more time with God.**

Now that you have read that, you may be worried. What if I don't like His desires for my life? I have yet to speak to a person on this topic that cannot relate to that question. It is human nature to want to be in control of our lives and it is difficult to phantom letting go of our dreams or trading our current dreams for unknown ones. The oldest sin in the Bible, and it is what brought Lucifer down, is the desire to be our own god. That same sin was committed by Adam and Eve and it is a sin we must fight against daily.

Let's look at a few things. God knew you before you knew you (Jeremiah 1:5). God created you for right now (Acts 17:26). God designed you with Himself as the blueprint (Genesis 1:27). His desires for your life will always and ultimately be a blessing for you. When you are seeking after the heart of God all things work together for good (Romans 8:28).

Motivations can be prioritized. For example, I am motivated to be comfortable. I would like to live a life of leisure where I can travel on a whim and enjoy spa treatments or weeks off relaxing by the beach at any given time. But my motivation to see my children walk in their purpose is greater than my motivation to be comfortable. I can do both, though I may not be able to do both at the same time. If I must choose one or the other, my children win. Motivations should bend, not break. The way motivators are presented in our lives may vary in presentation however, the roots of the motivator should be unwavering. The root of my motivator is love.

With this is mind, our emotional response to the world around us should be checked often and with vigilance. Once we've identified our true feelings, then measured them to determine if they line up to the standard, we should then check our motivation to realign our output with the standard. This requires our actions to change. Our motivation is why we adhere to the standard or blueprint for our lives.

My daughter Summer had some very cute, black, Mary Jane style shoes and they were too small. At the ripe young age of two years old Summer loved shoes, especially this pair, which she'd outgrown.

I was sitting on the couch watching her try to squeeze into those too small shoes. I'd tried explaining they were too small, they'd be uncomfortable if she'd gotten them on and though they were cute they were no longer good for her growing feet. This is when God tapped me on the shoulder.

Have you ever been in a comfortable place to long? Have you felt God prompting you to move? To go into a new season? To grow into something, means you grow out of something. I, like all of you, have a comfort zone. This place is cozy and comfortable, but every now and then things get too tight and then things change. Comfort and predictability serve as motivators to keep me where I am, even though I know it is time to move on.

> *God doesn't want you comfortable, he wants you thriving.*

The Israelites had a comfort zone and they were pushed way out of it. The cool thing is, where they were going was greater than where they had left. They were in slavery but had gotten comfortable operating in bondage. In the same way we get comfortable operating in sin. When they'd reached a point of discomfort, God created a way of escape and gave them the opportunity to obtain something better. Some of us are operating in relationships, jobs, or seasons we've outgrown but we try to remain in because it is comfortable.

God doesn't want you comfortable, he wants you thriving. He doesn't want you in bondage, He wants you to operate in freedom. He doesn't want you to be a borrower, He wants you to be a lender. God doesn't want you where you are, He wants you in the promise of where He is taking you.

Unfortunately, the Israelites that were freed from captivity, didn't enter the promised land. They could not let go of their comfort zone enough to go in; but you can. You can decide now, today, to leave where you are spiritually, physically, relationally, emotionally and decide to walk into God's promise for you.

You can decide to accept God into your heart and decide today to leave the comfort of sin and walk instead in the freedom of love. What God has for you is so much better than what you can get for yourself. Take off those uncomfortable shoes, God's got a new pair for you.

Our motivation cannot be fear. It cannot be fear of death, of loss or even of pain when measured against the love of God. Perfect love casts out all fear (1 John 4:18). This simply means that true love and fear cannot occupy the same space; we have to choose which one we will be motivated by.

This concept of checking my motivation has even affected the way I discipline my children. One day my little KJ got in trouble about 30 minutes before nap time. His consequence was that he was no longer allowed to play and had immediately to go to bed. He cried and screamed, calming down only to hear my decision and apologize. Then he asked me for cuddles.

"Cuddles?! Little boy don't you know you are in trouble? Don't you know what you did was wrong, and you made me mad?" Though it was just a moment, it was at this moment I had a choice to discipline or to punish my son.

See he already was informed about the consequence of his actions and he was experiencing that hurt. But would me withholding my physical affection be to further add to the lesson, or would it be in retaliation? To not give cuddles would be a response based out of my anger rather than my love, so, I "caved".

As I held him in my arms, I began to think of how familiar this situation is in my life. I've made decisions and suffered consequences, but God has never withdrawn his affection from me. Two scriptures whispered in my heart as I held this sweet, growing boy in my arms.

"I will never, leave you or forsake you..." Heb. 13:5

Even when I mess up, even as I am experiencing the results of my decisions?

"I will never, leave you or forsake you..."

Even when I scream and yell with my life, or when I throw a tantrum with my actions?

"I will never, leave you or forsake you..."

The other scripture I was reminded of was Romans 8:1 "There is therefore no condemnation to them which are in Christ Jesus, who walk not after the flesh but after the Spirit."

To condemn someone means to sentence them to punishment. My boy, who has not yet decided to live his life in Christ, sees my example of God's love. Through his 2-year-old eyes, he cannot discern discipline from punishment. So, I must teach him. Though his actions may cause some unpleasant reactions, God's love won't fail. This must be demonstrated through both my actions and reactions. Motivation, once identified, has the power to change the dynamics of even the simplest of your interactions.

CHAPTER 6

How to Lead with Motivation

The church should be motivated by one thing. The saving of souls. Our goal should be to make disciples of all nations. Matthew 28:19 says, "Therefore go and make disciples of all nations, baptizing them in the name of the Father and of the Son and of the Holy Spirit,"

It is clear, our purpose is to spread the gospel. It is not to have the most amazing worship team, or the most dynamic speakers. It is not to have an amazing children's ministry or impactful homeless ministry. Those things are helpful and may be motivated by the scripture above, but it is not the embodiment of it.

The reason for our existence as believers, is to share the good news of Jesus. We share this not only with our words, but with our behavior. Our culture is changing and as our laws and communities transform to include and even celebrate lifestyles that do not line up with the Word of God, some parts of the church lose their focus. They go from spreading the gospel, to defending it.

When I was in high school I used to argue about the existence of God any chance I got. I loved the rush I got from having a platform and proving my point. I would come home and recount my conquest in my mother's hearing. One day after my long and elaborate story my mother quietly responded, "Truth needs no defense." To this day, that phrase sticks with me. The truth can stand on its own. So it breaks my heart when we as a church respond to the world as if we have to fight it, rather than save it.

> **1 John 4:4** says, [4] You are of God, little children, and have overcome them, because He who is in you is greater than he who is in the world.

This scripture just makes my soul leap with joy. Greater is He who is in me, than he who is in the world. *No matter what the world says or has to offer, God is in me and He is more powerful than any force I can be presented with.* Can you see the power of the church? We have enough power to light up the world but are content using it to charge a cell phone. We cower afraid of the types of baggage people may bring with them when they enter the house of God rather than encouraging them to come and letting them know we have a place for all of that baggage.

We draw lines in our mind about what kinds of behavior we will and will not accept. We proudly uphold holiness, while forsaking than acting out of Christ love. Jesus wrapped himself in filthy flesh, took on our weakness, our sin, our unrighteousness, yet we as a church act as if we can "catch" sin by being around the unsaved. Greater is He who is in us, than he who is in the world.

As a church we need to welcome everyone in: the bigger the sin, the greater the testimony. Yes, we want to protect our children and ourselves and we should. We protect them by trusting God, implementing His word in our lives, and listening to the prompting of the Holy Spirit. We use wisdom and witness in teams (Mark 6:7), we set up safeguards to protect our children (Matthew 18:6) and we operate from a place of love, not fear. (1 John 4:18) If your motivation is not love then you need to change your motivation. Proverbs 15:1 "A soft answer turns away wrath."

My father tells this story. He and his friend Warren used to play basketball in the evenings. They loved the sport and it was a great way for them to witness to others. One night during a game, things got a little physical on the court. Warren was elbowed in the mouth by a player on the opposing team. They had to stop the game to allow everyone to cool down. After the game my dad and Warren spoke with the aggressive ball player. They told this guy about God and that God wanted a relationship with him. That night they took him to the church and baptized him in Jesus' Name.

They entered the court with their motivation in mind, to be a witness. Warren could have been offended that this guy purposely fouled him. He could have rightfully confronted the guy and gave him a piece of his mind. However, his motivation as a member of the body of Christ superseded the motivation of his own pride. They handled this situation with emotional intelligence. As a result of his integrity and commitment to his end goal; Heaven rejoiced at the addition of a new member to our family of believers.

As a church member, leader and/or mentor we must be wise in our dealings; mindful of our tone and volume. We should answer softly and peaceably whenever we can. A soft answer turns away wrath. (Proverbs 15:1) The tense atmosphere of a situation can be transformed by using the power of the pause.

Matthew 11:6 says, "Do not be easily offended." Let me give you some background on the story. John the Baptist was Jesus' cousin. He was his first friend. He was present before Jesus began His ministry, before Jesus was even born. John leapt in his mother's womb when she heard Jesus was coming. (Luke 1:41) John grew up and served as a herald for Jesus. He told all who would listen that Jesus was the Messiah. John even baptized Jesus. (Matthew 3:13-17)

In Matthew 11 John is imprisoned, he is about to be beheaded and his cousin is going through the country performing miracles. Can you imagine being in a cold, nasty jail cell because you are truthfully proclaiming that the King of Israel had arrived? Then that same King you are proclaiming, is not coming to save you. I would be hurt, sad, and furious.

John, discouraged and downtrodden sends a message to Jesus, "Are you really the Messiah, or are we waiting on someone else?" Jesus tells the messenger, "Go and tell John the things which you hear and see: *The* blind see and *the* lame walk; *the* lepers are cleansed and *the* deaf hear; *the* dead are raised up and *the* poor have the gospel preached to them. And blessed is he who is not offended because of Me." (Matthew 11: 5-6)

> **If Jesus told John the Baptist not to be offended I'm pretty sure that whatever you're holding on to, He wants you to get over it.**

Jesus told John how he was setting everyone free, but him, then tells him not to be offended. If Jesus told John the Baptist not to be offended I'm pretty sure that whatever you're holding on to, He wants you to get over it. He wants you to forgive and focus on growing the church. He wants you to make disciples of all nations. He wants your focus off on you and on to Him.

From the beginning of humankind's time on earth, we've allowed our personal desires to come between us and God. As a result, work became strenuous. Genesis 3:17 says, "Cursed is the ground for your sake in toil you shall eat of it, all the days of your life. Both thorns and thistles it shall bring forth for you and you shall eat the herb of the field. In the sweat of your face you shall eat bread until you return to the ground, for out of it you were taken; for dust you are and to dust shall you return."

We went from enjoying fruit as a result of God's labor to bearing the burden of working hard ourselves. I believe we were originally designed to live forever, basking in the presence of God. Our main job to communicate with Him as He met us in a beautiful garden. Instead we chose the knowledge of good and evil over the wisdom of being with God. Over time we dealt with murder, thievery, slavery, sin. This bondage, this burden of sin was to much to bear and we began to cry out for a savior. He came. His name is Jesus.

Matthew 11:28 Come to me all you who labor and are heavy laden and learn from Me, for I am gentle and lowly in heart, and you will find rest for your souls. For my yoke is easy and my burden is light." Jesus came with a light burden, an easy yoke. All He required was surrender. The realization that He is greater than we. He promised fulfillment, and everyday He delivers.

John 6:35 And Jesus said to them, "I am the bread of life. He who comes to Me shall never hunger and he who believes in Me shall never thirst." He rescued, He set free, He delivered and He fulfilled. When we accept that God is our substance we no longer have to fight the thorns and thistles for our bread. We accept that the hunger in our soul, is greater than the hunger in our bodies and we trust that the healer of our soul will provide food for our bodies.

Isaiah 48:17 say, God will teach us to prosper. Spend time with Him. He will show you things others miss. He will open doors that would otherwise be closed. You just have to decide that you will be motivated by His word, even when it goes against your instincts.

Philippians 2:5 Let this mind be in you which was also in Christ Jesus. The only way to have the mind of Christ is through prayer and the studying of His word. As we draw closer to Him, He grants our desires because His desires become our desires, His hopes our hopes. We learn His voice and respond to the promptings of the Holy Spirit. In doing this we find it is easier and easier to heed to His leading. 1 John 5:3 For this is the love of God, that we keep his commandments. And His commandments are not burdensome.

> *You are not acting saved because you are saved.*

Doing what God says is not burdensome! Thank God! We make things difficult when we try to duplicate results, rather than duplicate processes. There is no reason to act saved; it does not profit you anything but frustration. When you spend time with God, you let go of the things of the world. You let go of the desires of the flesh, because your desires are changed. For this reason, it is not burdensome to follow Christ. It is freeing! You are not acting saved because you are saved. You are simply being who God has designed you to be.

When our life is burdensome and when we begin to lose sleep over it, that's vanity. We are self-seeking, when we believe the things we are wanting to accomplish, can only be accomplished by our hand. We cannot save ourselves, if we could we would not need Jesus. The work of God is easy, and His burden is light, not because it doesn't take effort (if that were the case there would be no yoke at all) but because the majority of the effort and work responsibility is God's.

You may go through times of discomfort, frustration or even anger but that is not the rule for a believer, it is the exception. If you only do what God tells you to do, and only say what God tells you to say, the outcomes don't bother you, because God is not surprised. You know He has already prepared for the outcome and you had the privilege to be used by God for His purpose.

Once we are saved, we no longer have to eat bread with sweaty faces, because Jesus is the Bread of Life (Gen 3:17). Once we have Him, we satisfy our souls hunger (John 6:35). Our every desire can be satisfied by Christ but being human there are times we still seek our own way.

Let's examine the example given in scripture. A yoke connects a young ox with a stronger established ox to till and work the field. The stronger, often older, ox knows how and where to walk, to be successful at his task. The younger ox is pulled along in the beginning. The stronger ox sets the pace and direction. God is asking that we take His yoke upon us and learn from Him. (Matthew 11:29) When we allow ourselves to be pulled along we are submitting to the work of the stronger ox. If we start to go in a different direction then the ox we are attached to, we feel pain because the stronger ox cannot be moved.

When we comply, we are able to see progress and take pride in the fruit of our labor. The stronger ox does most of the work and other than being connected, the weaker ox is simply along for the ride. Over time, farmers could eventually remove the yoke when the younger ox was strong enough to be on his own, but thank God, He will always be the stronger ox and He will always be the one to take on the bulk of the work burden.

Our motivation should not be to separate from the yoke but to yield to it. When we spend time with God in prayer and scripture reading we are learning why He does things the way He does. These revelations should be documented and used to build our plans.

> **Habakkuk 2:2-3** Then the LORD replied: "Write down the revelation and make it plain on tablets so that a herald may run with it. ³ For the revelation awaits an appointed time; it speaks of the end and will not prove false. Though it lingers, wait for it; it will certainly come and will not delay.

I've learned that the closer you get to God, the more He answers, "yes" to your prayers. Not because He likes you more, but because the more time you spend with Him the more you begin to act like Him. The more you act like Him the easier your work becomes. The easier your work becomes the more effective you are at doing your work.

Our responsibility is not only to be motivated, but to motivate others.

If you are in a leadership/mentor role you need to have a clear vision to lead the people. When they read your vision, it should inspire them to act and spur them to invest in it. This doesn't always look like a financial investment it may be utilizing their resources to help your vision succeed. Your goal should be filled with passion and you need the skills and trainings to back it up. Our responsibility is not only to be motivated, but to motivate others.

We live in a time where we have information at our fingertips. If you don't know how to do something you can look up instructions online and you likely have someone in your network that can provide you with the support, you are needing. When you are motivated by the Word of God and you are lining up with what He is asking you to do. You will be equipped with all the resources you need. Everything you need to know will be at your fingertips.

As a wife, mother, caretaker, and teacher I have "busy" down. I know how to do busy. I can take on a million task willingly and sacrifice time, money and sleep to get things done. Unfortunately, one of the easiest things to overlook is my quiet time with God. It's easy to say going to services a few times a week, joining a daily prayer line and trying to commit my daily Bible verse to memory is enough, but the fact of the matter is, it isn't. That may seem like a lot but God, is calling us to intentional time with Him.

I will use marriage as an example because my husband is the most important person in my life. Imagine, if I only went out with him while in a group, included him in a group conversation and only knew His characteristics by the insights others shared based on their time with him. Our marriage would be fun at times, even enlightening, but it would be far from the truly intimate relationship I desire to have with him.

Imagine, He is asking me on personal dates, wooing me with flowers and even calling and leaving me sweet messages. My friends and family would think I was crazy for neglecting such an important relationship. If my husband offered me all his secrets that were guaranteed to change my life, in exchange for one on one conversations with him, it would be silly for me to pass that up.

How then is it okay to devalue our time with God? We should seek after Him like a bride stealing glances at her groom. Looking for opportunities to steal away. We should take His private messages to us as priceless heirlooms and though it is fun and enlightening to be with

Him in a group, we should value those private conversations above all else.

In Luke 10:38-42 Martha, frustrated, asks Jesus to reprimand Mary for sitting in His presence, rather than helping her serve the group. In verse 41 Jesus says, "Martha, Martha you are worried and troubled about many things." Busyness can equate to worry and being troubled. It is not God's will for us to be worried, in fact His word says the opposite. He instructs us to give Him our cares, because He cares for us (1 Peter 5:7).

If you follow God, you should not worry. Worry equals fear. Fear equals hiding or covering, more specifically burying. In Matthew chapter 25 we find a story about a man who paid a steep price for fear. A master (investor) gave three of his servants (think startups) different amounts of money. Two of the three came back with an increase. One servant buried what his master gave him, because he was afraid. As a result, he was killed.

> **Fear equals hiding or covering, more specifically burying.**

We cannot act in fear, it robs us of progress. When we, as a church body, adopt fear as our motivator, we are being robbed of an increase of brothers and sisters; along with what they have to bring to the kingdom of God. Fear goes against the nature of Christ. If we bury our talents, purpose, or callings, even if it is by doing good things, the result may be bareness, in a place where God intended there be fruit. So let's be intentional about opening our church doors despite our biases. He who is in us, is greater than he who is in the world.

There is only one way we, as believer, can bear good fruit. By spending one-on-one time with God. I will say this over and over again because it is my best advice, "Spend. More. Time. With. God." I had a friend ask me what my time with God looks like. Everyone is different.

I wish I could say, I start with worship, then spend time acknowledging who God is, thanking Him, talking about my hopes, and concerns, then asking His will. I would then read His word and just sit in silence waiting for Him to give me an impression. Then I would confirm if it is God by reading and studying His word.

This simply is not my reality now. Did I mention I am a stay at home, homeschooling mom of three and a caretaker for my grandmother? My time with God looks like trips to the grocery store, where I turn off the radio and ask God for guidance and grace. It is reading a few verses on my phone and asking God for insight as I give the kids a bath. It is reading the kids a Bible story before bed, only to discover that God was using that same story to confirm a decision I was having trouble making. God is not asking you to transform your life. He is asking you to fit Him into your life, so He can transform you.

Luke 10:42 tells us to choose the good thing. The good thing is spending time with God. Romans 8:14 lets us know, sons of God are led by His spirit. We can only be led, if we are connected. John 10:27 lets us know that if we are God's sheep we follow His voice. In order to know His voice we need to spend time with Him. 2 Timothy 2:15 tells us to study the word of God.

God wants to know us, and He wants us to know Him. God wants us to be motivated by Him. If what you are doing does not enhance your relationship with God, there is no good fruit in it. If there is not fruit in it, it is a waste of time. Your fruit is a good indicator of what motivates you.

Here are some questions for leaders

1. What is currently motivating you in your (Be Clear Habakkuk 2:2)
    A. Personal life?
    B. Professional life?
    C. Walk with God?

2. How can we pray with you concerning these areas? (Be prayerful 1 Thessalonians 5:17)
3. What tools do you need from us to assist you in executing the vision God gave you? (Be persistent Hebrews 12:1)

CHAPTER 7

Empathy

Empathy is the ability to emotionally place yourself in someone else's state of affairs. It is an important part of understanding how others think. The greatest example of empathy is Jesus. He loved us so much that He literally put himself in our shoes.

John 1:1 says, "In the beginning was the Word, and the Word was with God, and the Word was God. [2] He was with God in the beginning." Verse 14 says, "The Word became flesh and made his dwelling among us. We have seen his glory, the glory of the one and only Son, who came from the Father, full of grace and truth."

God has always wanted to be in a relationship with us. This is evident in Genesis. He created a place for Adam that had everything that would need, before He created him. He as the creator knew exactly what Adam needed and would need. He could see every molecule of Adam's being. He stood outside of time and watched the world from end to beginning and He still found value in being empathetic enough to become man to save man.

Seeing things from various perspectives is not empathy, it is sympathy. Empathy has a compassion element and it is coupled with the desire to know and understand what is being felt and not just why, but how. Jesus in all His compassion, put on flesh, in love.

In the beginning of this book, I defined emotional intelligence as, "the ability to control one's own emotions as well as the ability to influence the emotions of others". We have spoken at length about personal emotions, let's look for a moment at the emotions of others. The easiest way to identify the emotions of others, is to ask them how they are feeling and give them room to put words to those feelings.

Some people can answer right away, quickly articulating how they feel and why. Others may need to talk through their feelings, going through multiple options before settling on one. To effectively practice empathy, the one asking the question should patiently wait for the answer. Then be prepared to calmly and respectfully respond.

> **Empathy can be taught.**

Empathy can be taught. It is something that can be spurred through conversation and personal reflection. Empathy is best learned through experience. When we feel heard or understood there is a unique feeling, we feel called contentment. This does not always mean the problem is solved, or that we are okay with the situation we may find ourselves in. It simply means that in that specific moment we feel heard and are at peace.

When I was a little girl my mother told me a story.

Once upon a time there was a young girl who moved to a new area with her family. This also meant she was new to her school. Since she was a newcomer all the other kids would pick on her. They would make fun of her and point out her funny accent. They also teased her for wearing clothes that were different than everyone else's.

Every day the little girl would come home after school crying. She was heartbroken that she had no friends. Her mother hated seeing her this way so she prayed and asked God if just for one day he would turn her into a little girl, so she could be her daughter's friend. Her prayer was answered. The next day God turned her from an adult into a little girl, right after her daughter left for school. The mother turned little girl, then went to the school and acted as a student.

The other kids begin to make fun of her, they teased her about her clothes and made fun of her accent. They teased her because now she was a new student. The mother in the form of a little girl didn't mind, she was there for a purpose.

During recess, she spotted her little girl across the playground and as she made her way towards her. The other kids begin to chant hurtful things. The mother knew that if no one else was her friend, her daughter would be. As she made her way across the playground her daughter joined in the chanting. This made the mother very sad. Heartbroken the mother went home and waited to confront her daughter.

That afternoon her daughter burst through the door excited to tell her mother about her day. She explained that all the kids on the playground began to talk to her. They wanted to hang out with her, they wanted to be her friend. The mother calmly and quietly waited for her daughter to finish telling her about her day. She then said to her daughter, "I too had an interesting day."

She continued, "I prayed that God would turn me to a little girl so that I could be your friend. God answered my prayer right after you left for school this morning. I went on to the playground and I looked for you, but all the kids started saying mean things to me. As I started to walk towards you I knew you would play with me I knew you would be my friend. You joined in just like the others."

The little girl was devastated! She couldn't believe she'd been so cruel to her mother. She apologized and from that day forward she was the first friend of every new student at her school.

I thought my mother was telling me this story to teach me to be kind, but I realize now, she was teaching me to be empathetic. She was giving me tools through stories much like Jesus did with the parables. Through stories, my mother taught me to put myself in another person's shoes. She taught me, my perspective was a perspective, but it was not the only one. She also taught me to consider the group.

My mother is the second child of eight. Her mother was the oldest of five and her father was number 5 of 12. Their house was loud and busy and full of love. They learned to be considerate, kind, empathetic and to consider both the individual person and the group. My father, an only child, and mother went on to have five children, they continue this legacy of love.

Growing up, our house and van, were always filled with friends and family. Even when it came to the way we had church, we participated as a family. My siblings and I would lead worship on Sunday mornings. Gordon on the keyboard, my sister Amanda and I singing and my two youngest brothers Joshua and Christopher alternating on the drums. I would teach children's church and we would participate in lively discussions during Bible study.

These experiences lend to empathy. It was, through practicing interactions with each other, that we learned to appreciate the different ways people think. It also gave us a security. No matter what, we always had a place within our family.

Empathy is hard, especially in a culture that praises individuality, above the collective. In Western culture, success looks like big homes, where every child has his or her own room. It looks like following individual interests and pursuing individual goals rather than the goals of the group. Eastern culture leans more towards the collective. Measuring their individual choices against how they may affect all rather than one.

Empathy can be tricky, because it can also lead to assumptions or prejudgments. People with a high threshold of empathy, seem to have a low threshold for offense. They can usually explain away somebody's behavior, often giving them the benefit of the doubt. While people with low empathy, find it difficult to see past their own perspective. To be empathetic, one must be able to see beyond themselves. Understanding that everyone has their own issues they are working out. People's responses to an action or word, is a result not just of their feelings at the moment, but the baggage they carry.

> *People with a high threshold of empathy, seem to have a low threshold for offense.*

Once we recognize our emotions, regulate them, depending on the situation, and identify our motivation, we move out of the mindset of self, and into the mindset of others. When we can see things from the perspective of others, it makes it easier to change their perspective. It is important that as believers, we do not forget what we were saved from. The Bible tells us to compel them to come. (Luke 14:23) We are to convince or persuade others to receive the gospel of Jesus Christ.

When we recognize the motivation that lies behind behaviors, it makes it is easier to relate to the person that we are empathizing with. This means realizing, that we cannot always trust our hearts, or go with our gut.

Jeremiah 17:9 says, "The heart *is* deceitful above all *things,* And desperately wicked; Who can know it?"

If our gut goes against the Word of God, then we should follow the Word of God. Our gut usually goes with the choice that causes us the least amount of stress, so we can trust it to be self-preserving but not always God pursuing.

I like peace. I like things to go smoothly, people to be happy and everyone to get along. Naive? Maybe. Unrealistic? Definitely!

Sometimes I find myself in positions where I must disturb the peace. My peace.

When I pray, I ask for God's will to be done. I want what He wants, and I realize that doesn't always look like what I think it should. It does not require, my input, my peace, or my opinion. My faith and action however, are requested.

> **Matthew 10:34** says, "Do not think that I came to bring peace on earth. I did not come to bring peace but a sword. [35] For I have come to 'set a man against his father, a daughter against her mother, and a daughter-in-law against her mother-in-law'; [36] and 'a man's enemies will be those of his own household.' [37] He who loves father or mother more than Me is not worthy of Me. And he who loves son or daughter more than Me is not worthy of Me. [38] And he who does not take his cross and follow after Me is not worthy of Me. [39] He who finds his life will lose it, and he who loses his life for My sake will find it."

Doing what God wants always causes division somewhere. God wants to be our first love. He wants our desire to be with Him, to supersede our desire to connect with anyone else. He tells us to take up our cross and follow Him. To bear the burden to save others. If we give our life to Him, He will give us life in Him.

This is our cross to bear, to choose to step out of what is comfortable and to do instead what is right. To stand alone, if necessary, to follow Christ. Not hiding behind the authority of parents or the responsibility of raising children but deciding instead to choose Christ above all else. Doing this makes us better spouses, better parents, better sons, daughters and friends. Our motivation, constantly being checked against who we are trying to be, rather than who we are at the moment.

So how can you produce peace when you have none? Isn't peace a fruit of the spirit (Galatians 5:22-23)? Peace, real peace, not the superficial fleeting peace, based on feelings that change with the situation. Real peace is rooted in faith, that you are doing what God wants you to do and that if you aren't, God knowing your heart will correct you. Real peace is a reward for obedience, not a prerequisite for action.

CHAPTER 8

How to Lead with Empathy

Empathy within the church lies in the transparency of its leaders. When church members and visitors feel like their leaders can relate to them, they are more likely to share issues in their own lives. This opens the door for authentic relationships and deliverance. We overcome by the blood of the lamb and the word of our testimony. (Revelations 12:11)

Leaders should use wisdom when being transparent. It's important not to glorify past sins or exploits. So, when sharing, details may not be necessary. However, it is important to let congregants and most importantly unbelievers know: there was a change that occurred, as a result of Christ. If we always act as if we've always been saved, or our sins weren't as bad as some others, we negate the importance of salvation.

Every parent has or will experience a time, where their child is coming toward them with some filthy biological material covering them. When your child is running towards you, your first response is not to hold out your arms and prepare for an embrace. Your first response is to yell, "Wait!" or "Stop!" Once you stop them you start directing them towards the bathroom or someplace to bathe them.

You don't want them to touch anything, not even you. Once you get them where you want them. You start giving them directions. You may even carefully help them disrobe. You then clean them up and wrap them in a big fluffy towel.

Our sins are just like the biological filth in this story. We come towards a loving creator covered in sin. He tells us to, "Stop! Repent!" Once we recognize our state of being and its filthiness in comparison to the prestiness of Christ. We are directed to the next steps. Baptism, the filling of the Holy Spirit, the production of fruit, as a result of basking in the presence of God. Filth is filth! When we start to compare our sins with others, we glorify the wrong thing. Our conversation, instead, should be, "He took me too. He cleaned me up. He removed all the filth, and even though I get dirty sometimes, He takes the time to clean me up all over again."

The gospel spread so quickly in the Bible because people changed drastically as a result of being saved. Acts chapter 2 talks about how believers were filled with the Holy Ghost with evidence of speaking in other tongues. There was an immediate manifestation, an immediate evidence of change that allowed the unbelievers the faith they needed to believe. I'm convinced that if we are less focused on protocol and pomp and circumstance, and more concerned with sharing our testimony and forming relationships with people, we can make a remarkable impact as the Body of Christ.

The evidence of the infilling of the Holy Spirit in Acts was speaking in tongues. Though this evidence manifested immediately in Acts, there are cases where the evidence of the infilling of the Holy Spirit took time and prayer. I am reminded of William Seymour and the Azuza street revival in 1906. In February Seymour moved to Los Angeles and preached the power of the Holy Spirit, but It wasn't until a few months later in April 12th of the same year that Seymour received evidence of the Holy Spirit himself.

One thing I love about Seymour's story is his willingness to act and share what the Bible said was true based on the Word, not based on his personal results. Sometimes we have to act on what we know to be the truth, even if we have not yet seen it manifested in our lives.

Obedience sometimes proceeds provision, but God always pays for His order.

> **Obedience sometimes proceeds provision, but God always pays for His order.**

Relationships are difficult, especially now. We live in a time where someone can get almost any piece of information they want or desire without any real human contact. There is no fear of judgement or having to explain oneself. Without situations that cause us to stretch and cause us to expand our world, we become islands disconnected and hopeless. Our interactions become more and more ingenuine and complicated.

Interactions do not become complex in the sense of conflict, but rather in struggling with conversing face to face. The more disconnected from physical interaction we are, the more we struggle with forming and conveying authentic feelings, concerning any given topic. These things inhibit our empathy and the very judgment we fear from others, we begin to perpetrate.

Jesus shows us what real empathy looks like by inserting himself into a society with strong ideas, clear agendas, and a presumed identity. He introduces His ideas by reframing the concepts that were already in existence. For example, the Jews were expecting a literal king to come and deliver them. Jesus came to deliver them spiritually. He used scripture to explain who he was to the Pharisees, and they missed him.

One of my continued prayers is, "God please don't let me miss you." Jesus was right there talking to Pharisees, engaging with them, teaching them, debating with them and they had no idea who He was. They had no idea the significance of the time He was taking to be with them. I pray that God changes my eyesight, so that I am not blind to what He is doing in the Supernatural.

John 10:27 Jesus answered, "I did tell you, but you do not believe. The works I do in my Father's name testify about me, [26] but you do not believe because you are not my sheep. [27] My sheep listen to my voice; I know them, and they follow me."

Are you listening for God? God has placed unique gifts into each one of His creations. There is something to be done, that only you can do. There is someone who can only be reached by you, but to be an effective leader you must learn to be a good sheep. It's exciting to be in charge, to put together a plan or flush out an idea but unless we are followers of Christ, how can we empathize with others' difficulty to follow?

The manifestation of empathy is compassion. I love that Jesus always addressed the issue, THEN He healed it. When interacting with the world He fulfilled the physical need, then the spiritual.

> ### The manifestation of empathy is compassion.

Let's look at the story of the Samaritan Woman in John chapter 4. The Samaritan Woman was at the well during the hottest part of the day. It is assumed, she was there at a time when she would be alone. This woman was likely an outcast due to the number of husbands she had and the current company she was keeping.

The first thing Jesus did was ask her for something to drink. He reminded her that she had value. She had something to offer. Her baggage did not disqualify her. Even though she was a Samaritan woman, and He was a Jew in a time where the two did not get along. Even though she was a woman, who had multiple husbands, she still had a role in the kingdom of God.

The devil tries to convince people they don't deserve salvation. Guess what? None of us do. It is not something to be earned or something to be worthy of. It is a gift from an empathetic God. No matter how saved we act, or how many things we have been delivered from, we must not forget where God brought us from.

In John 4:10 Jesus offers something to the Samaritan woman. He wanted her to know that despite how the world viewed her, she was still worth receiving something from the Savior. My favorite verse is 17. It is here where He reveals to her, His compassion. He shows her that He is not partial to the opinions of others. He has not counted her out. He knows exactly who she is, He knows the baggage she carries, and He still believes she is worth it.

This is the only case in the Bible where Jesus brings up someone's sins before saving them. I believe He did so as an act of compassion. He wanted to show the Samaritan Woman that even in knowing who she was, what she'd done, and how others felt about her, He still found value in her. As believers we need to pray for discernment, so we can address the issues of the people and lead them to Christ.

In the Bible there were no miracles done in the temples, they were done in the streets. They were performed for people who knew they needed a savior, rather than for those who believed they had it figured out. We are God's hands and feet it's up to us to heal the land.

When looking at the church honestly and looking for ways to implement these concepts do not be discouraged. As I measure my church and my ministry against the words that I'm writing, I am forced to view them through the standard of the Word. Rather than feel defensive or discouraged, I feel empowered. I don't feel any stress or apprehension, because I know what ever state it is in, God is able!

I feel I can see things clearer than before, because I first measured myself against the Word. Having measured myself against the Word I have a level of compassion and understanding when looking at the way my local church operates and its ultimate motivation. This doesn't mean that I give the church a pass and accept things the way they are. What it means is that, I understand the church is built up of flawed people.

I personally need to be intentional with my relationships. I love that when we take the plank out of our own eye, we can see things with more clarity and are able to approach removing our neighbors spec with understanding. Taking the plank out of our eye helps us be compassionate. (Matthew 7:5) Another Biblical example of empathy is the story of the adulterous woman.

In John 8 the Pharisees brought Jesus a woman who had been caught in the act of adultery. The Pharisees wanted Jesus to comment on her punishment, which in that time would be stoning. Jesus simply said, "He who has not sinned, cast the first stone." Jesus could have cast the stone, but He didn't. He was showing us an example of empathy, asking us to put ourselves in the place of the woman, before passing judgment on her.

We live in a society where a whole lot of people, have a whole lot of opinions about things, especially the lifestyles of others. On both sides of the conversation you have passionate people who often times lack empathy. How frustrating it must be to believe with all that you are that what you feel is absolute and have somebody else come and passionately and venomously tell you that what you feel is wrong. How frustrating, it must also be to believe with all that you are that God has created things to be a certain way, and have somebody else tell you that your belief, that you feel is rooted in love, is rooted in hate.

> **It is not our job, to change people.**

God desires real relationships with EVERY person He has designed and there is nothing that can separate us from God's love. It is not our job, to change people. Our job as believers is to introduce them to Christ, walk them through salvation and disciple them on their journey. God does the changing. God does the transforming. The church belongs to Him.

Empathy in emotional intelligence is so important. People cannot be wholly defined by one aspect of who they are. The world labels and defines, but the Word of God says we are fearfully and wonderfully made, no qualifiers. (Psalm 139:14) The world tries to convince people that their decisions can qualify or disqualify them for salvation. We know that God knocks on the door of our hearts, again no qualifiers. (Revelations 3:20)

It is for this reason we need an unwavering standard. Feelings and beliefs change but if your standard is rooted, unmoving and secure, then we can look at it as the unchanging end goal.

Here are some questions you can ask your leaders.

1. What is your personal testimony (How do you know God saved you)?
2. When is the last time you shared your testimony?
3. How can you be intentional about being empathetic?
4. Do you only surround yourself with those who share your perspective? Why? Why not?

CHAPTER 9

Relationship Skills

The foundation of our creation, existence and survival is based on our ability to form and maintain relationships. God created us, to be in relationship with us. In order to maintain healthy relationships, we must at some level, be able to identify our feelings, examine and change those feelings if needed, uncover our true motivation and be able to put ourselves in another person's shoes. To form healthy relationships, one must possess some emotional intelligence and forming healthy relationships is a byproduct of emotional intelligence.

God uses relationships to teach us. When we are children, our parents and caretakers teach us how to interact with the world around us. They teach us the appropriate emotional responses for various situations we may find ourselves in. Whether our experience with them is good or bad, these first relationships in our lives set the precedent for how we engage in the relationships to follow.

I have a good friend who was raised in foster care. She didn't have loving parents, that told her the world was her stage. She had parents that neglected, abused, and abandoned her. As a result she developed a habit of proving herself valuable. Now as an adult she is one of the hardest working, most underappreciated people I know.

Her first relationships attributed to her development of weak boundaries. As a result, she was very emotionally aware but not very empathetic. She had trouble understanding the decisions of people who "had it all." This presented as judgmental and argumentative. God is redeeming those first relationships in her life and she is now setting clear boundaries, growing in confidence and she has strong relationships in her life, that both love and challenge her thinking and beliefs.

As a result, her emotional intelligence has greatly increased, in the time I have known her. She could have read about emotional intelligence in a book and taken no action which may have had a slight but not permanent effect on her life. By intentionally practicing emotional intelligence within her relationships, the emotional intelligence of all parties involved in her life has increased. The more diverse your genuine relationships, the easier it is to empathize with different people.

Racism is a touchy subject in our country. It colors, no pun intended, so many aspects of our society and effects the individual despite their background. Let's look at black and white relations for a minute. The term "white privilege" can put people on both sides into a fighting stance. A white person may hear this term and immediately want to debunk it. After all, they are not personally racist, and they have worked hard for everything they have.

A black person may hear the term and have many specific examples, about how this "privilege" has negatively impacted their life. The term simply means that there are more opportunities for one group than the other and history backs that up. I have found that whites who have a diverse group of black friends, have an easier time addressing and exploring this phrase. They notice the privilege and call it out.

In my experience, I have also noticed that blacks with a diverse group of white friends have an easier time explaining these complex terms with examples their specific audience can relate to. My point is, developing complex and diverse relationships increases your emotional intelligence because it increases your empathy. As a believer, empathy is vital to the spread of the gospel of Jesus Christ.

Relationships are organisms, that change with the impact and influence of the world around them. They are established with boundaries that change and evolve as the relationship grows. Friendships, marriages, mentors, siblings, peers, co-workers, acquaintances and even parent/child relationships utilize emotional intelligence. The level of emotional energy expressed to be empathetic, often correlates with the type of relationship.

> *Relationships are organisms, that change with the impact and influence of the world around them.*

I am more likely to take the time to consciously practice emotional intelligence when interacting with my spouse, children, or family members. I will take time out to intentionally pause or allow more room for explanation in an argument with them, than I would with an acquaintance or co-worker. As emotional intelligence is practiced it becomes a sub-conscious response. Our choices become habits, and our habits become character traits.

One day I had a friend over to hang out and catch up. In the middle of our conversation about good intentions. I heard the water running outside. I immediately knew it was my son who turned on the water.

I yelled out the screen door. "KJ turn off that water!"

"Okay mom!" He replies, and I heard the faucet being shut off.

A few minutes later I heard the water running again.

"KJ!"

"Yes mommy?"

"Is that water back on?"

"Yes." He sighs knowing he is in big trouble.

"Come inside and go get in the bed, until I come talk to you."

"I was just trying to water the grass," he mumbles as he comes in and goes to his room.

Concerned that my response may have seemed harsh and seeing myself in similar situations, where I got in trouble for just trying to help. I turned to my friend an explain to her KJ's position.

"I was just trying to water the grass. Afterall, it is the middle of summer and it is hot outside. The once green grass is now in patches in the backyard. The grass needed water. What is the big deal? I was being helpful. I was doing what needed to be done. I took initiative and now I am being punished for it. I don't understand."

As I went on and on she stopped me and said, "Okay, okay I get it."

This is how we are, when it comes to things, that God tells us not to do. We hear it all the time, "the road to hell is paved with good intentions." In fact, that phrase is one of my favorite quotes. The problem wasn't that he was watering the grass. The problem lied in his disobedience. He thought he could see and understand things I couldn't. He was mistaken.

Isn't this how we are with God. We see an opportunity and though God tells us to stop, wait, or move, we decide to do things our way. We know He is older than us, wiser than us, stronger than us, but we still want to do what we feel is right based on the information we have on hand. We almost can't control ourselves.

> **Isaiah 55:8-9** says, "For My thoughts *are* not your thoughts,
> Nor *are* your ways My ways," says the LORD. [9] "For *as* the
> heavens are higher than the earth, So are My ways higher
> than your ways, And My thoughts than your thoughts."

My sweet boy had forgotten, just a few days earlier as soon as the sprinklers were turned off a very large snake crossed the yard. He didn't have to engage or watch for that threat, so he could not comprehend its significance. He is not frightened of getting bit by a snake or concerned about whether or not a snake can get into the house. The threat has no relevance to him or impact on his life.

For me, the situation is much different. I am charged with the care, growth, and development of my son. It is my responsibility to keep him safe, to protect him from the threats that lie in wait. Even when the threat is me. As a parent to my children I am their greatest advocate, but my words and actions also have the potential to do the most harm.

Children make mistakes. They make a lot of mistakes. They are exploring the world, discovering the impact they have on their environments, and they are learning what works and what doesn't. For those of us who believe we understand how many things work, this can be very frustrating and at times overwhelming.

It is my responsibility to respond to the children in my care, in a way that will build them up, instruct them, and direct them. Not in a way that demeans or harms them. The adults in our home do not use words like stupid or dumb. We do not speak negative sentiments over our children and we do not speak negatively about them to others. Even in our frustration we strive to protect our children.

When KJ decided to water the grass, he did not realize that our state was in a drought and he had absolutely no idea, that the water he was frivolously using was a utility that needed to be paid for. In his mind he was doing the right thing. Our decisions can sometimes cost more than we realize.

We can act on impulse thinking we are doing something good, but I have learned that if the enemy cannot get you to do something bad, he will settle for busy. We can get so caught up in doing good things that we don't do "God things". As we draw nearer to God it is easy to get caught up in the trap of doing what we think God will want rather than seeking His will. Surely God won't mind if I water this grass, it needs to be done. All the while, we create circumstances that come with a price.

It blesses me so much when God allows me to see myself in my children, because once I see myself in them; I am better able to respond to them, as close as I can to the way God responds to me. This mirror in the eyes of my children, helps me to be both empathetic an intentional with my words and actions. It encourages me to be vigilant and I encourage their growth and development. God sends people to help us navigate this journey of life. They may see things that we don't see or understand things that we do not.

After the watering the grass incident, I was able to sit down with KJ and talk to him. I thanked him for taking initiative and trying to solve a problem he saw. This is a behavior trait I want to reinforce and see more of. I explained that he needs to obey me quickly and the first time because I see things he doesn't. Respect for authority is something he is developing. Finally, I gave him the opportunity to show me he learned from his mistake. I let him go back outside and play.

I applauded the behavior I wanted to see, I addressed the problem behavior and I gave him room to grow. This is also how we should interact with one another as peers. When we have an issue with someone, we should acknowledge that they are important. Simply because they are a human being. They matter to God. We should keep that fact in mind, when faced with challenging social interactions.

The Bible says this in Mark 12:31 [31] And the second, like *it, is* this: 'You shall love your neighbor as yourself.'[a] There is no other commandment greater than these."

My husband shared with me something God revealed to him during his quiet time. He said, "This scripture is not saying to do the things for your neighbor, that you would like but rather to do things for your neighbor that they like, as if you were doing for yourself the things you like."

He continued, "When we are arguing, I want to have a moment to myself. You want to solve the issue right away. Loving you like I love myself means loving you the way I want to be loved even when it goes against the way I want to do things. So I talk through the situation with you because that is how you feel loved."

This neighbor loving business is hard. It is more than being cordial with people we pass on the street, it is loving intentionally. Seeing a need and meeting that need. As my husband mentioned above, it can also affect the way we handle conflict. The Bible has instructions for that as well.

> **This neighbor loving business is hard..**

If we have a problem with our neighbor, we should address the problem with the intent to get it resolved. If we can't resolve it in a one on one situation, we should bring in wiser people to help us navigate through our issues.

> **Matthew 18:15-17** states it clearly "[15] "If your brother sins against you, go and tell him his fault, between you and him alone. If he listens to you, you have gained your brother.[16] But if he does not listen, take one or two others along with you, that every charge may be established by the evidence of two or three witnesses. [17] If he refuses to listen to them, tell it to the church. And if he refuses to listen even to the church, let him be to you as a Gentile and a tax collector."

We should take every chance we can to solve a problem. Sometimes this means simply looking at the person's intent and if their intent is noble letting it go. Other times this means sitting down with the person and letting them know they've hurt you. The intent of both parties should be to restore the relationship between the two of you. This peace and unity is important among both believers and unbelievers. Among believers unity bonds us.

> Paul says this in **Ephesians 4:1-6** "I, therefore, the prisoner of the Lord, beseech you to walk worthy of the calling with

which you were called, [2] with all lowliness and gentleness, with longsuffering, bearing with one another in love, [3] endeavoring to keep the unity of the Spirit in the bond of peace. [4] *There is* one body and one Spirit, just as you were called in one hope of your calling; [5] one Lord, one faith, one baptism; [6] one God and Father of all, who *is* above all, and through all, and in you[a] all."

When we are in unity with one another, we are operating the way God intended, supporting and connecting to one another. When we seek peace with unbelievers we create an opportunity to witness. This does not mean the result is peace, unfortunately martyrs die every day for the faith. It means you carry the peace of God when witnessing to unbelievers seeking opportunities to share with them the gospel of Jesus Christ.

As believers we should forgive, and forgive, and forgive. If we look again at Matthew 18, we see how many times we should forgive.

> **Matthew 18:21-22** "Then Peter came up and said to him, "Lord, how often will my brother sin against me, and I forgive him? As many as seven times?" [22] Jesus said to him, "I do not say to you seven times, but seventy-seven times."

I chuckle when I read this scripture, because I know some of us have people in our lives that make us want to count every time we forgive them. To remove the temptation from you to do that, let me share with you this passage of scripture.

> **Matthew 6:14-15** For if ye forgive men their trespasses, your heavenly Father will also forgive you: But if ye forgive not men their trespasses, neither will your Father forgive your trespasses.

Emotional Intelligence increases as we see ourselves for who we are. The most difficult steps in growing and using emotional intelligence, in my opinion, are self-awareness and motivation. It is so easy to do things without realizing why we are doing them. We get into a routine and pick up habits that are contrary to our goals. Sometimes, we make excuses for them by measuring ourselves against other saints or unbelievers; because those standards seem attainable.

> *Emotional Intelligence*
> *increases as we see*
> *ourselves for who we are.*

There is never a point in our relationship with Christ where we have arrived. Seasoned saints and even mega-church pastors have serious work to do when it comes to their relationship with Christ.

Philippians 3:12-16 states it plainly,

> [12] Not that I have already attained, or am already perfected; but I press on, that I may lay hold of that for which Christ Jesus has also laid hold of me. [13] Brethren, I do not count myself to have apprehended; but one thing *I do*, forgetting those things which are behind and reaching forward to those things which are ahead, [14] I press toward the goal for the prize of the upward call of God in Christ Jesus. [15] Therefore let us, as many as are mature, have this mind; and if in anything you think otherwise, God will reveal even this to you. [16] Nevertheless, to *the degree* that we have already attained, let us walk by the same rule,[b] let us be of the same mind."

I thank God that though I will never arrive at a perfected state, with each press towards Him, I am blessed with more and more of His presence. The more I am in His presence the more I realize how far from perfect I am. Perfection is not the goal; intimacy is.

For the past few years, I have unsuccessfully tried to grow a garden. (I will persist until I succeed.) Well one day, I realized I was growing a weed. I am not saying that a weed sprouted up alongside my plants I am saying I watered, tended to and actively grew...a weed! In an effort to grow some peppers and cucumbers from seeds I mistook this innocent looking weed as the start of a pepper or even a cucumber plant.

Let me back up a bit. A weed, as defined by a gardening friend, is a plant you did not intend to plant, growing. In other words, this was a weed because it was not bearing and would not bear the fruit I intended it to. You know God showed me myself. He revealed some weeds in my life I was actively tending to.

> **Galatians 5:22-23** says, The fruit of the Spirit is love, joy, peace, longsuffering, kindness, goodness, faithfulness, gentleness, self-control. Against such, there is no law.

I had to stop, meditate, and examine my fruit. I had some fruit in my life that was healthy and thriving, but I also had other fruit that I did not intend to grow. Those fruit did not look like the fruit I should have been growing, those fruit were weeds. I was not actively watering plants that would lead to positive fruit of the spirit. Instead in my absent-minded apathy, I'd begun to water and nurture some weeds.

Let me explain, I'd begun to compare my actual husband to my perfect imaginary husband. You know the husband that knows exactly what I want, when I want, and how I want it. The husband that takes cares of the kids, brings home the money, cleans the house and follows it up with romantic gestures. This imaginary husband was amazing but the fruit he bore was frustration and bitterness.

Then there were the children. My children were too much. Too loud. Too busy. Too kid-like. I wanted them to be statues that I could dress up, download information into and expect them to perform on demand. The fruit this bore was impatience.

I was busy. I had a lot going on. I was too busy to read the Word, too busy to take time to hear from God, too busy to be grateful. My boundaries were blurry, and my heart was exhausted. My plan was not written, and I was overwhelmed. The fruit was misery.

I'd realized what I was doing by examining the fruit of my weeds. This is not what I wanted! I wanted gentleness, faithfulness and goodness. I wanted peace and long- suffering. I wanted kindness and joy. I wanted fruit that would attract lasting spiritual results not fruit that would eventually destroy my resolve.

I was taking time, energy, and intention to care for weeds. My husband was not going to get away with not meeting the impossible standard set in my mind. I was not going to let him treat me any old kind of way. He was going to know how blessed he is to have me. Another man would love a wife like me.

My children were going to learn to act like 30, maybe 40 years old with good sense, instead of the 6, 4, and 1 year old they were. They were going to sit still and be quiet. They would learn how to behave appropriately (as an adult) or they would be in big trouble. These kids are not going to embarrass me!

I was going to look like I had a lot going on even IF God intended for me to be still, after all I needed to keep up appearances. I needed to be the envy of my friends and the goal for strangers. My hair needed to be perfect, I needed the latest gadgets and the trendiest make-up. I will be superficially loved and desired. Everyone will want to be my friend. I will find my validation in acceptance from man instead of God. My weeds were bearing fruit and they needed to be uprooted.

The next part was simple. Repentance.

That word means admitting fault. It means making a commitment. It means deciding to be conscious of future actions, to prevent falling back into old habits. Yes, repentance is simple but difficult. Repentance takes emotional intelligence. It means addressing root issues, honestly, and at times painfully. It means recognizing the standard and recognizing that the standard is being missed. It means challenging motivations, behind actions and changing those motivations to match up to the standard. It means being empathetic, and seeing my past weaknesses in others, so I can share with them God's amazing grace. God uproot these weeds!

I had to with the help of the Holy Spirit intentionally pull every one of those weeds. When I started to daydream about what perfect husband would say or do, I replaced that thought with the gratitude for what actual husband did. As a result, I began to see more of his amazing attributes, than faults. I began to recognize how hard he works, and how much he sacrifices for our family.

My husband is an only child. I am the oldest of five children and family is very important to me. We are with my family every day. For a man who is used to having his own space, this is a challenge for my husband. I know it's a challenge because I know him, but he does not complain. Pulling weeds of comparison, strengthens our relationship, because I am able to see my husband honestly. He may not be my perfect imaginary husband, but he is my perfect -for-me, real husband.

When I started to get impatient with my children I would try to savor the moment and appreciate the innocent way they see the world and I would be intentional. I began documenting our homeschool lessons on social media. Listening to my kids tell their friends about how fun school is and looking back on past activities that worked really well helped me water the fruit patience and joy. As a result, my children enjoy learning and they are learning how to be patient and kind themselves.

I would be intentional in my spiritual growth. I would seek out God's presence and study His word. Being with God, taking out time to write the things He is showing me in His word is so exciting and rejuvenating. I can feel my spirit being watered with every word read and typed. I'm reminded of His faithfulness and love and I am overwhelmed with gratitude.

> *I would repent again because a garden full of weeds is not an option.*

When I failed at watering my fruit. When I began to water weeds. When I help others water their weeds. I would repent again because a garden full of weeds is not an option.

CHAPTER 10

Relationship Skill within the Church

The early church was based on surrender to Jesus Christ and built on trusting, intimate friendships. These believers were on the run, they were spreading the gospel of Jesus Christ like a wildfire while trying to avoid death or persecution. They had no choice but to depended on each other for emotional support as they watched their friends and loved ones killed for their faith.

After the death, burial, and resurrection of Jesus Christ, Christians were hunted. In fact, the Apostle Paul formally known as Saul of Tarsus was one of the people who hunted and killed Christians. Acts chapter 9 tells the story of his conversion. Paul was near Damascus when he was blinded by a light from heaven. He then heard the voice of God. Those traveling with him heard the voice but did not see the light. Their sight remained intact.

Right there, God created a situation where each party had something the other did not. Saul had to depend on the men he was traveling with. Immediately changing the dynamic between them. I believe based in the information provided about Saul and the way God spoke to him that he was likely the authority figure in his group. He had to go from giving orders to being led. From speaking and expecting immediate action to having to respond immediately to his subordinates' words.

Emotionally intelligent leaders trust those they work with to know how to do things they don't. If you as a leader are the smartest person in the room, you have the wrong people in the room with you. The church is filled with various parts of the body of Christ and every single person has something valuable to offer. Pastors and leaders are not the complete body of Christ they are components of it. Though they may act as the head of the church they are not the head of the Body of Christ.

If you as a leader are struggling with having control, not oversight but control, over every aspect of the ministry you may be suffering from pride and it will show in your leader's inability to delegate. Leaders follow, the leader they are following. If you don't trust your leaders, you set the precedent for those leaders not to trust those who work with them.

Our responsibility as Christian leaders is to serve. Jesus came and served. His miracles served the people He was healing. His teachings provided answers to questions the people needed answered. He did not come and proclaim that as the Son of God the people serve Him. This is what confused the Pharisees. Kings have subjects that respond to their every whim but this guy from Nazareth was proclaiming to be the King of Kings, while acting as a servant.

> **God uses relationships to humble us.**

God uses relationships to humble us. In order to lead as Jesus did, we are to approach leadership from the position of servanthood. We commit to serving God AND his people. Our job is to love like Jesus, so we follow his example.

> **John 12:49** "For I have not spoken of myself; but the Father which sent me, he gave me a commandment, what I should say, and what I should speak."

Jesus only said what his father told him to say. We should follow suit and seek God in everything we do.

HOW TO LEAD WITH EMOTIONAL INTELLIGENCE

As Saul was dealing with his sudden blindness in Acts chapter 9 God was speaking to Ananias. God asks Ananias to open his home to Saul, telling him that he has already sent him on his way there. Ananias reminds God of Saul's crimes against the church, yet God does not waiver and tells Ananias that Saul is chosen.

> **that God uses relationships to teach us to trust Him.**

Ananias must choose to put everyone he knows, in what he perceives to be harm's way to follow God's instructions. God gave him a few days' notice. He could have run, he could have gathered all his friends to hide, but Ananias decided instead to obey God. Being a believer can be fun and daring. When you are in communication with God, things are far from dull. Ananias reminds me that God uses relationships to teach us to trust Him.

It is not only the unbeliever that struggles with the choice to follow God. As believers we may be placed in situations that force us to choose, to preserve our flesh, or pursue the gospel. Years ago, our church prayed over a family who was moving to Cambodia. They were moving there as missionaries, to help fight human trafficking. They opened a center for young children they rescued from sex slavery. The thing that makes this family stick out in my mind and prayers is the fact that they too had young children.

This wonderful family was choosing to go to a hostile place and disrupt the economy of some very dangerous and morally repulsive people and bring with them the target of these criminals' enterprise. They boldly proclaimed that this was what God was calling them to do and to date they have rescued hundreds of children from this horrid industry.

So, Ananias obeyed God and embraced Saul as his brother in the faith. He not only obeyed God he did so fearlessly. His obedience helped Saul see again.

Acts 9:18 says, "Immediately what looked like scales fell from Saul's eyes." *God uses relationships to heal us.*

When we obey God the miraculous happens. It is not something we should be surprised by, we should expect it. We should respond to the voice of God with excitement and expectation. God is not frivolous. His words create universes. We have gravity only because He said it should be. After Saul's encounter with Ananias, Saul was baptized, filled with the Holy Ghost and became an Apostle of our faith. God then changed his name to Paul.

Paul used emotional intelligence in the way he shared the gospel, taught church leaders and mentored Timothy. We see the Apostle Paul's self-awareness in his transparency.

> **Romans 7:15** says, "I do not understand what I do. For what I want to do I do not do, but what I hate I do."

Apostle Paul lets us know that he is powerless against his flesh, it is the power of the Holy Spirit that gives him strength to resist sin. His self-awareness is something we see throughout his letters to the church as he offers wisdom and guidance without pretending that he himself is the standard.

While writing to the church in Philippians in chapter 3 verse 12 Paul admits he is not perfect he is just chasing after the things God has set before him. It is refreshing to hear church leaders remind congregants, that they too, need Christ still. I remember while working in the youth department years ago our Youth Pastor asked us, the leaders under him, to lay hands on and pray for him.

This stuck with me for many reasons. He trusted that the same God that was in him, was in us. He showed us that we didn't have to pretend we were okay, just because we were leaders. He also taught us the importance of staying prayed up, in case we were called upon to pray for him or any other leaders as needed. He was not afraid of us messing it up. I don't know if he knows or realizes the impact he had on the way I lead today but I am grateful that God used him to show me a picture of effective ministry leadership at that time in my life.

Apostle Paul shows us what self-regulation in the church looks like. In Romans chapter 1 he opens the book introducing himself, as a slave to Christ. Paul made clear that his standard, and the explanation of the standard that was established by Christ Jesus held rule over his life. Describing himself as a slave, he placed the lowest value on his life and the highest value on the Word of God. This man was educated at the top schools for his time, he traveled and established churches and then described himself in the lowest possible status of that time. A slave.

Paul's motivation was clear, to spread the gospel. His motivation outlived him, and he intended that to be the case. Paul took on a mentee, Timothy to ensure that his teachings would continue. He recognized that what God was doing in his life was special, but it was not exclusive, and it was not limited to his lifetime. If he wanted it to have a legacy, he had to set a foundation and move it forward.

Paul was empathetic. He spoke to the churches from a place of knowing, he described own righteousness as filthy rags. He constantly placed himself on level or below those he was teaching. He did not speak to them as a spiritual authority but rather a mouthpiece of God. A slave, just repeating what he was told. A beggar, showing other beggars where to get bread.

Timothy and Paul are one of my favorite relationships in the Bible. Paul was a great leader and mentor to Timothy and as a result Timothy stood by his side while he built the various New Testament churches. Paul included Timothy so much in his work, that in Philippians he started opening his letters with greetings from them both. This simple action lets us know that the people of the church to whom he was writing were familiar with he and Timothy's relationship.

Paul was grooming Timothy to continue the gospel after him. As a leader our work should always continue even after we're gone especially concerning the ministry. A great example of leaving a legacy is found in the story of Abraham.

Abraham was told that he would be the father of many nations in Genesis 17:4. He was given this promise as an old man, in fact his name was Abram which meant father and he had no kids. God then changed his name to Abraham which means father of many. His name was changed, as a response, to the promise that God spoke on his life. Even though he had not yet seen the evidence of that promise, every time someone spoke his name, it was a reminder of how God operates.

When we hear a word from God, concerning the thing that he has called us to do with our lives, we should respond as if that thing is happening right now, in this moment nad we should plan as if we will not see the results. As Abraham was raising Isaac, he passed down the promises of God. When we look at Exodus 3:6 God spoke to Moses He said, "I *am* the God of thy father, the God of Abraham, the God of Isaac, and the God of Jacob. And Moses hid his face; for he was afraid to look upon God."

God identified himself by his relationship to Moses' ancestors. Look at how God speaks to the generations, through the generations and to generations past. He is intentional about establishing generational fruit.

Paul takes the same approach concerning Timothy. Even though Timothy is not his blood relative, he introduces Timothy as his son in the faith (1 Timothy 1:2). He was not simply Timothy's pastor in the sense we see in today's Western churches. He and Timothy really knew each other, and he groomed him to continue his work.

Through Paul's letters to the church, we see that Timothy is empowered as Paul encourages Timothy to continue even without him. 1 Timothy 4:12 says, "Let no man despise thy youth; but be thou an example of the believers, in word, in conversation, in charity, in spirit, in faith, in purity."

Paul understands that Timothy is going to have to speak to the church while he is still young, because at this point he has been arrested so many times he knows it's only a matter of time before he is killed for the sake of the Gospel. Rather than concern himself with his mortality, he focuses instead on a grooming Timothy to take charge of the mantle.

I come from generations of serving God. My family, through the generations has been many denominations, but one consistent thread that lies in our family is being called to spreading the Gospel of Jesus Christ and being called to serve. My parents are pastors, my grandparents on my mother's side still serve their local church in different ways, and my great grandparents were a pastor and a pastor's wife. They established a legacy of faith and unwavering commitment to God. When my great grandma, Mary, was a young lady she got very sick. Her father used to read to her The 91st Psalm every single day.

> [1]"He that dwelleth in the secret place of the most High shall abide under the shadow of the Almighty.
>
> [2] I will say of the LORD, He is my refuge and my fortress: my God; in him will I trust.
>
> [3] Surely he shall deliver thee from the snare of the fowler, and from the noisome pestilence.
>
> [4] He shall cover thee with his feathers, and under his wings shalt thou trust: his truth shall be thy shield and buckler.
>
> [5] Thou shalt not be afraid for the terror by night; nor for the arrow that flieth by day;
>
> [6] Nor for the pestilence that walketh in darkness; nor for the destruction that wasteth at noonday.
>
> [7] A thousand shall fall at thy side, and ten thousand at thy right hand; but it shall not come nigh thee.
>
> [8] Only with thine eyes shalt thou behold and see the reward of the wicked.

⁹Because thou hast made the LORD, which is my refuge, even the most High, thy habitation;

¹⁰There shall no evil befall thee, neither shall any plague come nigh thy dwelling.

¹¹For he shall give his angels charge over thee, to keep thee in all thy ways.

¹²They shall bear thee up in their hands, lest thou dash thy foot against a stone.

¹³Thou shalt tread upon the lion and adder: the young lion and the dragon shalt thou trample under feet.

¹⁴Because he hath set his love upon me, therefore will I deliver him: I will set him on high, because he hath known my name.

¹⁵He shall call upon me, and I will answer him: I will be with him in trouble; I will deliver him, and honour him.

¹⁶With long life will I satisfy him, and shew him my salvation."

My great grandmother got better even though the doctors felt at times that she wouldn't make it. Later on in life she married my great grandfather. Not long after that, she was pregnant with my grandmother. The doctors told her that having this baby would put her life in grave danger. She decided to go ahead and have my grandmother anyway. My grandmother Carol Gordon was on the missionary board at Bethel AME for over 30 years.

About another year passed before she was pregnant again this time with my uncle, the doctors gave her the same warning letting her know that this delivery could take her life and cause her child great harm, but she believed God and she had my great-uncle. Cornelius Austin, became a great minister and pastor.

After that she was pregnant again, this time with twins! The doctor told her that if she did not terminate this pregnancy she would surely die, she gave birth to two beautiful baby girls, my great-aunt's. Noella Buchanan and Arvella Strong became pastors and are still active ministers.

Finally, another year passed she got pregnant with my Uncle Wellington who was a deacon in the church until he passed away. In each of these pregnancies she was faced with the decision to trust what the world told her was reality, or to trust the word that was spoken over her life as a girl.

She held strong to her faith, and served as such a beautiful example of God's faithfulness. During most of her life she was either a pastor's daughter or a pastor's wife, she was always surrounded by faith. She would laugh, as she told this story reminding us that in God's faithfulness, joy can be found. At 95 she went on to be with the Lord but her legacy for the generations to come has been firmly established. God will call you to something that will outlive you. Be bold, be humble, and be prepared, your legacy will be great because God is great and you submitted your life to Him.

The best example of emotionally intelligent relationships in the Bible is Jesus. He formed relationships while still in Mary's womb. He had parents, He had siblings, He had cousins, and He had disciples. Even His word reinforces the importance of relationships. John 13:35 "By this everyone will know that you are my disciples, if you love one another."

The world would know the disciples, based on their relationship with people. Jesus taught His disciples how to truly love others. He spent quality time with them, He sacrificed everything for them then He filled them with His power.

You can measure the emotional intelligence of a church by the love church members and leaders show to visitors. When church leaders are excited and loving, they create an environment that others want to be a part of. This consistent environment creates a culture This culture should line up and support the vision of the church and support the word delivered from the pulpit.

> **When church leaders are excited and loving, they create an environment that others want to be a part of.**

It is easy for unbelievers to write off the message of Jesus when they are feeling attacked from the pulpit. I don't condone watering down the Word of God or changing the message to suit the desires of the flesh. In fact, I propose we spread the word the way Jesus did. Jesus met the need first. If the people were sick, he healed them. If they were hungry he fed them. He answered questions, he told stories, he formed relationships.

Jesus never stood in front of His followers, and thanked God He wasn't in their condition. The Pharisees did that. The longer you are in church the easier it seems to fall into the belief that the church is your "place of worship" rather than a place to introduce unbelievers to Jesus. When we receive the Holy Ghost, when God takes up residence in our hearts then we become the physical embodiment of the church. The place we call "the church" is simply a meeting place; the power of God is in the believer.

When people are around us they should feel the love of God. Our self-awareness should be measured against God's love. We should regulate ourselves to better show the love of God. Our motivation should be to show God's love, and finally we should be able to empathise with those searching for God's love and give it to them freely. If sharing the love of God is not the end goal, then our work is for naught (1 Corinthians chapter 13).

If we want to teach the Word of God, our lives must be that example and to do that we must love each other. The church should be the place people see relationships work. It should be the model for sisterhood, brotherhood, families, friendships and marriages. After all, "the one who is in you is greater, than the one who is in the world." 1 John 4:4

It breaks my heart that the statistics for lasting marriages is the same inside the church as it is outside the church. I believe real, authentic relationships can remedy that. When we approach each other, only with the intent to show authentic love, then it becomes harder to become offended. We would automatically give people the benefit of the doubt and try to empathize with their reason for doing things.

> *It's important we don't let the world dictate our actions or reactions, we need to be the change we want to see.*

It's important we don't let the world dictate our actions or reactions, we need to be the change we want to see.

> **Romans 12:2** "And be not conformed to this world: but be ye transformed by the renewing of your mind, that ye may prove what is that good, and acceptable, and perfect, will of God."

We need to walk in God's will. God desires for us to be emotionally intelligent. He wants us to be a safe place for His people. To do that we must renew our minds by remaining in constant communication with Him. We must seek a relationship with Him above all else.

Questions you can ask your leaders:

1. How has God used relationships to help you on your salvation journey?
2. How is He using you to help others on their journeys?
3. Is your ministry, auxiliary or small group a loving, hospitable environment for visitors?
4. How has God used relationships to help you on your salvation journey?

Conclusion

Emotional Intelligence is the ability to control one's own emotions as well as the ability to influence the emotions of others. When we practice self-awareness, self-regulation, check our motivation, practice empathy and are intentional with our relationships we open the door to live lives of impact. Our goal is to impact the world by winning souls for Jesus Christ. Utilizing Emotional Intelligence gives us the tools to show the world what a believer looks like.

As you were reading I pray you've resolved that being a church leader does not always mean you hold an official position in a local church. It means you are delivered and set free, the chains of sin are broken from your life and you are committed to seeing others set free as well. You can take these concepts, apply them to your life and share them with others.

Self-awareness is vital to the salvation process. We cannot be saved until we know we need saving. We must first recognize who God is and that we need Him. "Jesus said to him, "I am the way, the truth, and the life. No one comes to the Father except through Me." In John 14:6. We need to see ourselves and submit ourselves to the savior Jesus Christ.

Once we identify how we feel and recognize there is a standard, we should measure our lives against, we use self-regulation and respond to our feelings with our actions. Acts 2:38 says, "Then Peter said to them, "Repent, and let every one of you be baptized in the name of Jesus Christ for the remission of sins; and you shall receive the gift of the Holy Spirit."

Once our behavior is identified and regulated our motivation is changed. Now we want to follow the Word of God and share this freedom with others. Matthew 28:18-20 "And Jesus came and spoke to them, saying, "All authority has been given to Me in heaven and on earth. [19] Go therefore[a] and make disciples of all the nations, baptizing them in the name of the Father and of the Son and of the Holy Spirit, [20] teaching them to observe all things that I have commanded you; and lo, I am with you always, *even* to the end of the age." Amen.[b]"

Now that we are set free we can empathize with those who are not. Remembering how we felt and building relationships with a foundation of love, communication and understanding. Sharing our story with others, showing them real change occurred in our lives and compassionately and prayerfully introducing them to the one who can fulfill all their needs; is empathy in action.

> **Mark 12:30-31** And you shall love the LORD your God with all your heart, with all your soul, with all your mind, and with all your strength.'[a] This *is* the first commandment.[b] [31] And the second, like *it, is* this: 'You shall love your neighbor as yourself.'[c] There is no other commandment greater than these."

Finally, we have established our relationship with God. We are sharing the gospel of Jesus and we are growing in emotional intelligence. All the while we are a part of a beautiful community of believers. The Body of Christ. Romans 12:10 As the body grows we grow through prayer, Bible reading, and discipleship. Content in the unchanging love of God.

Be blessed.